# Pluralistic Therapy

*Pluralistic Therapy: Distinctive Features* offers an introduction to what is distinctive about this increasingly popular method. Written by one of the co-founders of pluralistic therapy, and a leading UK figure in counselling and psychotherapy, this book describes 15 theoretical features and 15 practical techniques for practitioners. Pluralistic therapy is a flexible, integrative approach to counselling and psychotherapy, which has also found applications in fields such as mental health, life coaching and careers guidance.

*Pluralistic Therapy: Distinctive Features* will provide an essential guide to students and practitioners of psychotherapy, or an allied area of practice, who are open to learning about new ideas and techniques from current interdisciplinary research.

**John McLeod** is Professor 2 in Psychology at the University of Oslo, and Professor of Counselling at the Institute for Integrative Counselling and Psychotherapy, Dublin.

GW00771194

# Psychotherapy and Counselling Distinctive Features

Series Editor: Windy Dryden

The Counselling and Psychotherapy Distinctive Features series provides readers with an introduction to the distinctive theoretical and practical features of various therapeutic approaches from leading practitioners in their field.

Each book in this series focuses on one particular approach and guides the reader through 30 features – both theoretical and practical – that are particularly distinctive of that approach. Written for practitioners by practitioners, this series will also be of interest to trainees, social workers and many others outside the therapeutic tradition.

**Titles in the series:**
*Pluralistic Therapy* by John McLeod
*Cognitive Analytic Therapy* by Claire Corbridge, Laura Brummer and Philippa Coid

For further information about this series please visit:
https://www.routledge.com/Psychotherapy-and-Counselling-Distinctive-Features/book-series/PCDF

# Pluralistic Therapy

## Distinctive Features

## John McLeod

**With Compliments**
**Devon Counselling**
**College**

Routledge
Taylor & Francis Group

LONDON AND NEW YORK

First published 2018
by Routledge
2 Park Square, Milton Park, Abingdon, Oxon OX14 4RN

and by Routledge
711 Third Avenue, New York, NY 10017

*Routledge is an imprint of the Taylor & Francis Group, an informa business*

*British Library Cataloguing-in-Publication Data*
A catalogue record for this book is available from the British Library

*Library of Congress Cataloging-in-Publication Data*
A catalog record for this book has been requested

ISBN: 978-1-138-20283-2 (hbk)
ISBN: 978-1-138-20289-4 (pbk)
ISBN: 978-1-315-39826-6 (ebk)

Typeset in Times New Roman
by Apex CoVantage, LLC

For Julia

# Contents

# Acknowledgements

I deeply the appreciate many conversations with colleagues who have allowed me to learn from their experience and understanding concerning the nature of flexible, collaborative ways of being a therapist: Bud Baxter, Kirsten Benum, Anne Marie Bourke, Caroline Burke, Mick Cooper, Windy Dryden, Miriam Finnegan, Marcella Finnerty, Gary Fox, Allen Gilhooly, Josie Gough, Hanne Haavind, Margrethe Seeger Halvorsen, Shay Hogan, Dorothy Ingram, Triona Kearns, Lizzie Lumsden, Thomas Mackrill, Lynsey McMillan, Dave Mearns, Christian Moltu, Katie Nicoll, David O'Regan, Michael O'Rourke, Hanne Weie Oddli, Helene Nissen-Lie, Siobhan Quinn, Marit Råbu, Sissel Reichelt, Steff Revell, Kate Smith, Kat Stevens, Rolf Sundet, Gillian Taylor, Mhairi Thurston, Ode Arne Tjersland, Jillian Walls, Dot Weaks, Mark Widdowson and Marguerite Woods. The editorial team at Routledge have been a consistent source of support: Joanne Forshaw, Kristina Siosyte, Kerry Boettcher and Jennifer Fester. My biggest debt, as always, is to my family: my wife Julia, my daughters Kate, Emma and Hannah, and my treasured granddaughter Eva.

# Introduction

The main principle of pluralistic therapy is that people who enter therapy are experts on their own lives. They have a deep implicit understanding of what they need to help them to move on in their lives, when they need it and how it might best be delivered. People also have a sense of what they don't know and need to learn. From such a starting point, a therapist is faced with two key challenges: how to enable the client to articulate and apply his or her own personal knowledge; and how to bring their own massive stock of professional knowledge into the picture in a way that augments and does not crowd out the client's strengths and resources. In pluralistic therapy, the strategy for dealing with these challenges is the adoption of a collaborative style of working, grounded in a commitment to transparency and shared decision-making.

All forms of therapy are broadly similar, operating through a set of 'common factors' such as instillation of hope, practising healing rituals, acquiring a rationale/way of making sense of life difficulties and the development of a connection with a trusted and culturally recognised healer. A pluralistic approach is therefore similar to other therapies in most respects, forming one way in which these factors can be articulated. However, all models of therapy can also be viewed as possessing distinctive features that reflect novel and innovative variants on a common therapeutic process. The aim of this book is to highlight the distinctive features of pluralistic therapy – how it represents one particular style of 'plain old therapy' (Allen, 2012, 2013). Following the format adopted in other texts in the Routledge *Distinctive Features* series, the book is organised around brief accounts of 15 distinctive conceptual and theoretical aspects of the approach, followed by a description of 15 ways in which pluralistic therapy is distinctive in practice.

The second half of the book includes an anonymised case study that runs through all of the chapters. The intention here is to provide a concrete example of how pluralistic therapy works in practice.

Pluralistic therapy comprises a "meta-theory" or practice framework that functions as a means of harnessing the ideas, knowledge and experience of both the client and the therapist. Rather than being restricted to change interventions from a single approach, a pluralistic therapist draws on whatever concepts, skills and techniques are available to him or her. A pluralistic therapist may be someone with primary training and experience in cognitive behavioural therapy (CBT), psychodynamic therapy, person-centred/experiential therapy, narrative therapy or in some combination of these (and other) traditions. A pluralistic framework for practice comprises a set of principles and procedures for shared decision-making around how to proceed in therapy. It is a framework that allocates space for the unique, vital, creative coming together of the client and the therapist, including making use of relevant resources from the cultural worlds within which they live.

As an approach to therapy that emerged in the mid-2000s, pluralistic therapy has had the advantage of being able to build on a rich body of findings of therapy research studies conducted over more than a half-century, encompassing investigations of all types of therapy. One of the consistent and robust findings to have emerged from therapy research is that it is the therapist, not the therapy approach, that makes a difference. The variation in outcome attributable to different therapists is substantially greater than the variation attributable to therapy models. In the light of these findings, one of the key distinctive features of pluralistic therapy is that it is designed to help therapists to make the most of what they know, avoid errors, align themselves to the needs and preferences of each client and engage in a process of continuing learning and development.

Pluralistic therapy takes account of the context in which it is carried out. For example, the scope to negotiate length, frequency and number of sessions, and flexibility around scheduling, are factors that depend greatly on the particular policies of different agencies and clinics. In addition, the ingenuity and creativity of therapists and clients, alongside the pace of social and technological change, means that new therapy ideas and practices are emerging on a regular basis. For these reasons, pluralistic therapy is best regarded as an open system. The capacity to re-invent itself in response to changing circumstances can be viewed as a criterion for evaluating the success of pluralistic therapy and the enduring relevance of its underlying principles. Readers – both clients as well as therapists – are encouraged to approach the ideas in the present book as an invitation to consider the relevance of particular pluralistic concepts and practices for their own learning and development, rather than as constituting a fixed system to be adopted as a whole.

At the heart of pluralistic therapy are three key images. The first is an image of the client as the hero of therapy (Duncan, Miller and Sparks, 2004). It is the client who has the courage to break away from self-undermining ways of being, thinking and relating, and experiment with new possibilities. The therapist is merely a companion, a guide, a teacher, a carer, a provider of resources for the client over one stage of their journey. The second image is that of a responsive therapist who has a range of things to offer, is morally committed to making the best possible use of their talents in the service of the other and views each client as a unique other who affords an opportunity to learn more about the human condition. The third image is that of the improviser, the artist, the designer, the bricoleur. Even when drawing on established and well-understood therapy ideas and methods, both client and therapist strive to achieve moments of creativity when something new, some shift in perception of feeling that fits and seems right, emerges and becomes apparent.

Much of the practice of pluralistic therapy involves strategies for maintaining an effective alignment between what the therapist can offer and what the client can use. From a pluralistic perspective, the limitation of almost all of the established approaches to therapy is not that their ideas are wrong or that their techniques are ineffective, but that these ideas and techniques can only be helpful if they are sufficiently aligned to pathways that the client is following already, or that make sense to the client as viable and credible alternatives.

In seeking to create a framework for therapy in which the client and therapist can work together, it is essential to be sensitive to language. In pluralistic therapy, the aim is for each case to generate its own shared language, in the form of idiosyncratic and personal word choices, images and metaphors, that resonate and have meaning within the client–therapist relationship. In order to support this aspect of the work, pluralistic therapy does its best to avoid technical language and made-up terminology. The sections in this book are anchored in everyday language, such as goals, tasks, methods, collaboration, understanding, decisions, dialogue and preference. These are ideas that are familiar to most people.

It is important to point out the limitations of the present book. It focuses solely on individual therapy, and does not address the application of a pluralistic approach in couple therapy or group work. There has not been space to explore the challenges associated with specific client issues such as depression or eating problems. Some significant aspects of the thinking behind pluralistic therapy are only briefly mentioned: the necessity for therapists to be informed by a cultural and political perspective, the complex question of the relationship between research and practice, the nature of therapist training and professional development and the relevance of an appreciation of unconscious processes. It is essential to keep in mind that the case example in Part 2 of the book represents only one way in which pluralistic therapy can be practiced – there are many varieties of pluralistic therapy that exist, depending on the background, knowledge and interests of the therapist and the setting within which he or she works.

# DISTINCTIVE *THEORETICAL / CONCEPTUAL* FEATURES OF PLURALISTIC THERAPY

1

# A brief summary of how pluralistic therapy works

The idea for pluralistic therapy emerged from an appreciation of four key findings that have been established on the basis of more than 50 years of research into counselling and psychotherapy:

1   There are many effective ways of dealing with emotional, psychological and behavioural problems in living. There are lots of things that help.
2   People who enter therapy are already actively involved in trying to sort out their problems. They possess significant knowledge, insight and preferences around what they think is most likely to be useful (and not useful) for them.
3   Therapy is more effective when it takes account of the client's preferences and their understanding of what helps. Therapy that is not informed by the client's preferences has the potential to be destructive and even abusive.
4   Therapy is more effective when the relationship between client and therapist is characterised by collaboration, caring and trust.

Pluralistic therapy provides a framework for harnessing these factors in the interest of helping clients to live more satisfying and productive lives.

In pluralistic therapy, it is assumed that both the client and the therapist have ideas about what might be helpful. In the case of the client, these ideas are based on personal experience, observing how other people cope with difficulties and learning derived from reading, watching movies and accessing other similar sources of information. It is likely that, for the client, much of this knowledge is implicit and that it will take time and support for him or her to articulate and make use of it. By contrast, therapists have a wealth of ideas about therapeutic processes, readily available to consciousness. Therapists also possess important personal knowledge based on life experience that may also make a vital contribution to the process of therapy. For both client and therapist, some of the relevant knowledge that they possess will refer to activities outside of therapy (cultural resources such as art-making, sport and exercise, spiritual practice, etc.) that may be activated in the service of therapeutic change.

The process of therapy involves the careful weaving together and application of therapist and client ideas. From the start, the pluralistic therapist tells the client that the client's ideas about what might be helpful are crucial, and that they are the only one who can tell whether what is happening in therapy is making a positive difference to their life.

Over the course of therapy, in order to ensure alignment between client and therapist inputs to therapy, the therapist initiates collaborative discussions around the goals and tasks of therapy, the methods/ interventions used to accomplish tasks and the way that the problem is being understood. These discussions are facilitated by the use of specific strategies that are central to pluralistic therapy practice. The therapist asks *direct questions* (example: 'What do you want to get from therapy? How would you like things to be different in your life by the end of our time together?'). The therapist uses *metacommunication* as a means of facilitating reflection on client and/or therapist intentions and reactions (example: 'I noticed that you made a shift there – you had been talking about difficulties in your marriage and then you seemed to switch to talking about your situation at work. Can I just check what was behind that, for you? Are they both part of the same broader issue, or was there some other reason?'). *Feedback measures* are used as ways of opening up discussion around the progress of therapy. A further means of ensuring effective client–therapist alignment occurs through *collaborative case formulation*, in which client and therapist work together to build a conceptual model of the client's problems, and derive an action plan.

The concept of a therapeutic *task* plays a central role in pluralistic therapy. Typically, client goals, such as 'moving on from the loss of my partner' or 'being more confident and assertive in work situations' tend to define a somewhat broad agenda. In order to make progress around that agenda, it is necessary to break it down into achievable sub-goals, or tasks. For example, in a client seeking bereavement counselling, progress in respect of the goal of 'moving on from the loss of my partner' could involve the accomplishment of tasks such as 'expressing and sharing how I feel', 'developing new friendships', 'finding ways to keep a place for the deceased partner in my life' and 'decisions around practical issues such as what to do with his possessions'. From a pluralistic perspective, there are always likely to be different techniques (methods) through which a task can be completed. For example, 'expressing and sharing how I feel' can be pursued through talking to the therapist, talking to other people, expressive writing, two-chair work, drawing a picture and many other strategies. The aim in pluralistic therapy is to find the method that works best for a particular client at that point in their process. Structuring therapy around the attainment of specific tasks ensures that what is happening in (and between) sessions remains focused on the attainment of therapy goals.

Pluralistic therapy emphasises the significance of the client–therapist relationship. From a pluralistic perspective, the process of therapy is not viewed in terms of the relationship *or* therapy techniques, as comprising separate factors. Instead, everything that happens in therapy has *both* a relationship dimension *and* a method (i.e. facilitating learning and change) dimension at the same time. A key concept in pluralistic therapy is the idea of 'collaboration' (colabouring, working together to build something, making use of the distinctive knowledge and skills of each co-worker). Each element of pluralistic work, for example identifying goals, metacommunication, collaborative case formulation, using feedback measures and other processes, represents action that contributes to building a relationship.

Rather than conceptualising the client–therapist relationship from a single point of view, for example as an 'alliance', a pluralistic perspective calls for consideration of multiple forms of relating. Different clients may respond best to different ways of relating, the same client may need different ways of relating at different times and each therapist possesses a limited relationship repertoire. The concept of 'alignment' refers to the degree to which therapist and client are pointing or moving in the same direction, whatever that might be. It is the job of the therapist to maintain alignment.

The client–therapist relationship is grounded in an ethical commitment to valuing the other person as unique. For the therapist, the connection that develops with the client is accompanied by a sense of moral responsibility for the well-being of the client and to do right by them. The underlying first principle that informs pluralistic therapy is that the therapist cares about the client as a fellow human being.

A pluralistic approach to therapy facilitates client learning and change in two main ways. First, it strives to ensure that the best change methods available to client and therapist are brought to bear on the client's problems. It does this by seeking to create the conditions for both therapist and client to make the most of the strengths and resources carried by each of them within their personal repertoires. Second, the experience of engaging in dialogue, collaboration and shared decision-making provides the client with a template for effective self-management and ways of relating to others that are productive and satisfying.

Pluralistic therapy does not claim to be more effective than any other approach to therapy, in terms of primary outcomes such as reduction of symptoms of anxiety, depression and so forth. What it does aim to achieve is to engage with and hold on to clients by taking their preferences seriously and explaining and negotiating what is happening at each step of the therapy process. This is a significant outcome given high dropout rates in most therapy clinics. It is also a socially and culturally inclusive approach to therapy, in terms of openness to different worldviews and belief systems, a structure for therapy that routinely addresses issues of difference and a purposeful embrace of the cultural resources of the client. As a way of doing therapy that specifically seeks to build on and refine the existing knowledge, resources and skills of the client, it has the potential to leave clients in a better position to cope with future life crises. The clinical and research evidence that is currently available can be found in Cooper and McLeod (2011), Cooper et al. (2015) and Cooper and Dryden (2016).

The following chapters expand on this brief summary by examining some of the key concepts or ways of thinking that support it.

2

# Pluralism

One of the defining characteristics of a pluralistic approach to therapy is that its roots are not in psychology, but that it is grounded in a philosophical concept: pluralism. Within philosophy, pluralism refers to the idea that there is no single correct answer to central questions of human existence. Historically, pluralism represents a key aspect of a gradual movement away from monist or single truth ways of thinking about the world, such as Christianity or Islam, in the direction of a perspective that acknowledges that it is not possible to attain an absolute or fundamental 'truth', and that one of the unavoidable challenges of being human is to live with uncertainty. A pluralistic stance is associated with a reflective and nuanced approach to the issue of epistemology – how do we know what is true? A pluralistic perspective implies that there are different types or sources of knowledge, each of which has its own validity.

The concept of pluralism makes it possible to highlight a major tension within prevailing theories of psychotherapy. At a values level, psychotherapy is, for the most part, distinctively pluralistic in adopting an inclusive attitude, exhibited in respect for client differences in such areas as religious belief, sexual orientation and political ideology. On the other hand, most psychotherapy theories base their explanatory models on one or two core concepts or change processes. These theories are non-inclusive, denying the relevance of competing ways of thinking.

By contrast, placing a philosophical understanding at the heart of the approach makes it possible to remain open to the significance of all psychological ideas and models. Established therapy approaches that highlight specific psychological concepts such as 'emotion' (Emotion Focused Therapy), 'cognition' (cognitive therapy), 'rationality'

(Rational Emotive Behaviour Therapy) or 'person' (person-centred therapy) create forms of practice in which certain ideas and areas of experience are prioritised over others. For example, some therapists focus their efforts on emotions, while others attend to cognitions. A pluralistic perspective makes it possible to see that human beings are characterised by *both* emotional *and* cognitive ways of relating to the world (and other ways as well).

A pluralistic philosophical perspective to the practice of therapy opens up new strategies for working with clients, through the use of a 'both/and' rather than 'either/or' way of thinking. Pluralism can be regarded as a way of 'thinking about thinking'. For example, when assessing a client, it may emerge that he or she is struggling with specific behavioural issues (such as panic attacks) and a pattern of self-destructive relationships. One response to such a pattern might be to conceptualise a treatment plan in terms of adopting *either* a cognitive behavioural therapy (CBT) approach that addresses the panic *or* a psychodynamic/interpersonal approach that addresses the relationship issues. In contrast, a pluralistic perspective invites consideration of how to work with the client in a way that attends to *both* the symptoms *and* the more general way of being. Pluralism therefore stimulates interest and curiosity in the existence of apparent opposites, polarities and dilemmas in the life or way of thinking of the client and the therapist.

One of the leading philosophical writers on pluralism, Rescher (1993), suggested that dissensus rather than consensus presents a defining attribute of what it means to be a person. Cultures, relationships and lives that are meaningful and generative are organised around ongoing conversation around what is 'right' or 'true'. These dialogues and debates never resolve into a single 'right' answer. In therapy, this insight leads to a realisation that one of the things that can be helpful for people is to be offered opportunities to engage in conversations that explore all available and plausible options in the search for a specific solution. Quite apart from the value of such conversations in relation to the particular issue that has led the person to seek therapy, it can be useful for some clients to learn this mode of talking and thinking as a general life skill.

Pluralism heightens an awareness that experience is punctuated by an endless succession of choice-points, where different possibilities may be considered. The practice of pluralistic therapy involves routinely inviting the client to reflect on the choices that are available to them at key moments in therapy, for instance in relation to what they want to get from therapy (goals), what would be best to work on right now (tasks), how to make sense of the issue being explored (understanding) and what would be the best way to tackle the task in hand (method). These reflective episodes within the ongoing flow of therapy have the effect of maintaining the alignment of the therapist to the client. They also have the potential to allow the client to develop a generally more reflective, collaborative and consultative approach to dealing with difficulties and challenges in their day-to-day life. To be able to work in this way, pluralistic therapists need to learn a way of talking that incorporates such elements as metacommunication, pauses, checking-out, tentativeness and hedging.

A final implication of the adoption of a pluralism as an organising principle for the conduct of psychotherapy lies in the domain of the professional identity of the therapist, and more concretely what a therapist reads, who they talk to and which traditions and disciplines they engage with. For the most part, psychotherapy is embedded in the disciplines of psychology, psychiatry and neuroscience. Pluralism opens up a wider set of intellectual resources in fields such as ethics, philosophy, social anthropology, sociology, history, politics and theology.

3

# Theory

Pluralistic therapy was developed at a point in the history of psychotherapy when a massively wide range of therapy approaches had already been devised and were in everyday use. In addition, several decades of psychotherapy research, conceptual analysis and integrative initiatives had failed to arrive at an agreed or consensus theory of psychotherapy. From a pluralistic perspective, this state of affairs is to be expected. In traditional societies a single way of understanding life, usually religious, was maintained through a rigid system of hierarchical control. By contrast, in contemporary society there exist spaces in which a multiplicity of views can be developed. The internet and globalisation make it possible for people to access ideas and practices from different cultures. We do not regard it as at all unusual for a person to seek to manage their anxiety or depression through a combination of medication, yoga, diet, self-help books and therapy.

Pluralistic therapy treats the diversity and multiplicity of psychotherapeutic theory and practice as a resource, and it espouses a critically appreciative attitude to all existing models of therapy. Pluralistic therapists are open to existing ideas and methods and actively curious about their practical value. At the same time, existing theories are not taken at face value but are regarded as products of particular social, cultural and individual influences. It becomes important to be able to view therapy theories as serving a number of different functions (McLeod, 2013, chapter 4). For example, psychodynamic theory may provide a therapist with a framework for making sense of complex patterns of behaviour and emotion in their clients. It is also likely to be highly personally meaningful in terms of helping the therapist to make sense of their own life, resulting in a strong personal attachment to the theory. Theory also functions as a language that gives access to a professional community.

Training in pluralistic therapy incorporates the development of skills around dismantling and reassembling mainstream therapy approaches and using existing theories as narrative structures that can form the basis of shared understanding with clients (Hansen, 2006). Pluralistic practice involves working with the client to identify the assumptions and types of story that the person uses to make sense of their life and experience. It may then be that the client comes to realise that their existing way of understanding incorporates strategies that can help them address current life difficulties. Alternatively, the client may be open to new narratives and perspectives suggested by their therapist.

Within this learning process, pluralistic practitioners develop a sensitivity to the relevance of the ways in which meta-theoretical perspectives/cultural traditions/discourses (e.g. feminism, democracy, ecology, science, art) have shaped not only prevailing models of therapy, but also the values and stances expressed in their own lives, and in the life choices of their clients. Pluralistic therapists are able to engage in 'internal pluralism' in the form of inner self-dialogues around alternative ways of making sense of issues. These dialogues may draw on internal conversations between different theoretical positions, or between different ways of knowing, such as personal knowledge and cultural knowledge. In order to engage in such activity, pluralistic therapists need to develop theoretical literacy through training experiences and private study and reflection that enables them to metabolise (Betan and Binder, 2010) or personally 'own' ideas and methods from across the landscape of therapy. This is a process that continues over the course of a career (Jennings and Skovholt, 1999).

By looking at the history and overall structure of psychotherapy theory and practice as a whole, it is possible to see that existing therapy approaches represent more or less arbitrary collections of concepts and interventions that have tended to reflect the personal experiences and social circumstances of their founders. Research into client beliefs and preferences shows that therapy theories do not map onto client theories in a straightforward fashion. For example, a client may make sense of their problems as arising from faulty thinking (CBT theory) while also believing that it is important to take account of what comes up in their dreams (psychodynamic theory). In pluralistic therapy, the aim is to activate the client's resources, including their ways of making sense of things. This requires being responsive to the client's implicit theories.

Research into the process of psychotherapy, and the interventions used by therapists from different approaches, suggests that there exists a core of 'common factors', such as instilling hope, offering a healing relationship and encouraging the client to express emotion, that can be observed in all approaches. At a more micro level, specific moment-by-moment therapist actions or interventions, such as offering an interpretation, challenging the client or making an empathic reflection, also occur in all therapies. From a pluralistic perspective, established theories of therapy offer interesting and informative ways of understanding different ways in which common factors and micro-skills can be deployed for different purposes.

A key distinctive aspect of the use of theory in pluralistic therapy is that it involves a shift away from thinking about theory as a fixed structure and guide to action that in some sense reflects 'truth'. This is replaced by a pragmatic interest in the process of 'theorising' – using ideas to build frameworks for understanding in particular circumstances in ways that open up possibilities for productive action (Swedberg, 2016).

4

## Context

On the face of it, the field of psychotherapy appears to be divided into two broad camps. 'Purist' approaches, such as cognitive behavioural therapy (CBT), psychodynamic, person-centred, existential and narrative, tend to be based on a single change mechanism or key idea. By contrast, 'integrative' approaches seek to combine ideas and methods from several (or all) purist approaches. Within this distinction, pluralistic therapy can be categorised as an integrative approach.

The aim of this section is to offer an account of the similarities and differences between pluralism and other integrative therapies to psychotherapy. However, before turning to that task, it is necessary to acknowledge that, from a pluralistic perspective, the purist–integrative distinction is not entirely satisfactory. The history of psychotherapy demonstrates that all approaches to therapy that are currently considered to be 'pure' models are actually assemblages of ideas and methods that were in circulation at the time they were founded. For example, Freud worked in a professional and intellectual culture in which concepts of the unconscious, life force/libido, a distanced type of doctor–patient relationship and interpretation were well-known. Key figures in psychotherapy, such as Freud, Rogers and others, can be seen to have created highly effective and persuasive syntheses of ideas and methods that were available to them. An important way of making sense of the difference between 'purist' and 'integrative' approaches to therapy is that the former have achieved brand recognition while the latter are either seeking to become recognised, or represent the work of individual clinicians who are just seeking to do the best they can for their clients, and are not interested in marketing their ideas.

A further important aspect of this issue, which is often neglected, is that from the beginnings of the establishment of psychotherapy as a recognised specialist profession in the 1930s, there has existed a line of argument that the purist–integrative distinction is unhelpful, and that all therapy is one thing (Duncan, 2010). This idea is in fact reflected in the rationale for the series of books in which this volume is published. All therapies are broadly similar in how they function, but possess distinctive features that reflect the particular cultural contexts within which they operate. These distinctive features can also be viewed as representing aspects of practice to which those operating within a particular approach have devoted time and effort, in the form of research, critical analysis and innovative practice. Over time, the best of these distinctive features gradually become more widely understood and accepted, and part of what all therapists do. For example, Carl Rogers paid particularly close attention to the process of empathic engagement with the client and the importance of a genuine relationship in ways that were convincing to colleagues from other therapy traditions and have influenced their work.

The purist–integrative way of thinking that dominates current therapy discourse has had the effect of reifying 'brand name' approaches and problematising efforts to innovate. Defining the process of innovation (small steps) as 'integration' makes any movement away from mainstream purist approaches look like a hazardous and challenging activity. By contrast, from a pluralistic perspective, the defining characteristic of mainstream therapy approaches is that each of them draws on a limited subset of change strategies, and denies the client access to methods that might help them.

At the present time, the main strategies for therapy integration are assimilative, theoretical, eclecticism, technical eclecticism and common factors (McLeod, 2013, chapter 17). Assimilative integration occurs when a therapist is trained in one approach and gradually introduces new ideas and interventions into their repertoire. Theoretical integration occurs when a new approach is built around a combination of concepts from existing approaches, through forming conceptual bridges across different sets of ideas. Eclecticism refers to a way of working in which the therapist chooses what is best. Technical eclecticism is a form of eclecticism in which the therapist uses a set of principles for making such decisions. Finally, common factors integration refers to the idea that all therapy approaches include the same core elements, such as a therapeutic relationship, a rationale and so on. While each of these strategies makes sense, it seems clear that none of them is sufficient in itself – each of them appears to describe one among many possible pathways of innovation.

A pluralistic stance invites reflection on whether additional pathways could be identified. Other types of therapy integration or innovation highlighted by McLeod and Sundet (2016) include *holistic integration* (the therapist seeks to develop an understanding of himself or herself as a whole person), *disorder-specific integration* (ideas and interventions are brought together to respond effectively to the needs of a particular client group), *multicultural therapy* and *feminist therapy* (therapy that is responsive to particular sets of values) and *collective integration* (therapists work together as a team, possibly including colleagues from other professions, to offer the client a range of therapeutic possibilities).

Pluralistic therapy incorporates all of the integrative pathways outlined earlier (McLeod and Sundet, 2016). Given the prevailing influence of the purist–integrative distinction, it makes practical sense to describe pluralistic therapy as an integrative approach. At the same time, pluralistic therapy represents a critique and rejection of the underlying assumptions that inform current debates around integrative versus purist therapy. What are currently regarded as single or 'pure' theories of therapy can be seen as partial or fragmentary approaches that systematically disregard change processes that are known to be helpful. Pluralistic therapy is a version that Allen (2012) usefully characterises as 'plain old therapy' (POT), by which he means the best efforts of front-line therapists to respond constructively to the needs of their clients or patients. From that perspective, pluralistic therapy seeks to take POT forward by attention to elements such as collaboration and the involvement of the client in shared decision-making; activation of potential change processes, including the use of extra-therapy cultural resources; and recognition of the ethical or moral dimension of therapeutic practice. Pluralistic therapy is therefore integrative in the sense of working towards expanding POT by integrating ideas from cultural studies, moral philosophy and shared decision-making in health care.

5

# Ways of knowing

Epistemology refers to such issues as the criteria that are used to evaluate the truth of statements and, more broadly, the worldview that underpins not only a person's way of making sense of experience, but also their *way of knowing* the world (Bruner, 1986).

There have been many attempts to clarify different epistemic styles or ways of knowing. The 'world hypothesis' framework suggest that there are four distinct positions: seeing the world in terms of black/white categories (*formism*); a *mechanistic* way of thinking that regards the world as a machine; a *contextual* mode of understanding that makes sense of events as arising from cultural and historical circumstances; and an *organic* worldview that views events in terms of growth and wholistic patterns (Lyddon, 1989). Alternative perspectives on ways of knowing make distinctions between rational, empirical and metaphoric ways of understanding, between individualist and collectivist ways of being or between narrative knowing (stories) and paradigmatic knowing (if–then abstract theories). It is also relevant to consider philosophical traditions such as objectivist/realist, social constructionist and spiritual/transcendental. Related ideas can be found in the literature on multiple intelligence and learning style.

There is evidence that therapists are attracted to theoretical models that match their personally preferred epistemic style, and that client preferences for therapy interventions similarly match their worldviews (Lyddon, 1989; Neimeyer et al., 1993).

A further way of making sense of ways of knowing can be found in McLeod (2016). This is based on the notion that therapists and clients are able to draw on five contrasting sources of knowledge: theoretical, practical, cultural, personal and scientific. While each source provides a valuable means of making sense of issues, each of them possesses its own strengths and limitations. As a result, the most effective problem-solving occurs when dialogue takes place between different ways of knowing.

A pluralistic stance acknowledges that we live in a culture marked by multiple truth criteria and multiple worldviews, and that the clients with whom we meet may be guided by worldviews that differ from our own, or may be struggling within their own lives to reconcile epistemic styles that are in conflict. *Epistemic fluidity* therefore is a distinctive aspect of the conceptual framework of pluralistic therapy: practitioners seek to be responsive and respectful around different ways of knowing, and to flow between them as necessary. For example, a client may be fearful of exploring his problems in depth because he defines personal problems as either 'solvable' or 'symptoms of mental illness', and further categorises the latter as too awful to contemplate. His therapist, by contrast, does not see where the difficulty lies; she makes sense of the client's issues as arising from life experience (contextualism) and regards a medical-model diagnostic approach as just one among many cultural discourses that might be relevant. It is likely that this tension is not trivial. It is not merely a matter of differential access to information about therapy treatment options, but instead reflects an underlying difference in ways of seeing the world, that would probably be exhibited in respect of any topic that was being discussed. The challenge here for the therapist is to be able to de-centre herself from her preferred worldview in order to engage with a worldview with which she is not familiar, and may even dislike.

In pluralistic therapy, cultivating epistemic fluidity is not an abstract intellectual exercise, but instead represents a necessary skill in relation to the capacity of aligning with the underlying worldview and problem-solving style of the client. A relatively straightforward way of developing epistemic fluidity is to become aware of different sources of knowledge that feed in to therapy practice: personal, theoretical, practical, cultural and scientific/research-based (McLeod, 2016). Dilemmas and choice-points within the therapy process, for example issues that are taken to clinical supervision, tend to be associated with disjunctions between two or more ways of knowing.

A simple example of how epistemic fluidity can be incorporated into therapy practice can be found in the work of the Australian psychotherapist Mark Pearson (2011; Pearson and O'Brien, 2012), who invites clients to complete a multiple intelligences questionnaire (at home), and then uses time in a session to discuss with the client any potential implications of their problem-solving patterns for the way they might best work together in therapy.

Concepts such as worldview and epistemic style refer to psychological and philosophical ways of making sense of this phenomenon. However, in practice, these aspects of the person are often most strikingly associated with social and occupational categories. For example religious fundamentalists, musicians and scientists are likely to exhibit contrasting epistemic styles.

It is instructive to compare pluralistic therapy with problem-solving therapy (Nezu and Nezu, 2013), an approach that shares an emphasis on identifying client goals and helping clients to generate their own best ways of accomplishing these goals, and which represents a valuable source of ideas and methods that can be incorporated into pluralistic therapy. Problem-solving therapy is based in a single epistemological position, an objectivist perspective grounded in neuroscience. While coherent in its own terms, this way of thinking limits the ways that therapists and clients make sense of issues, which has the effect of limiting the possibility of dialogue and the kinds of solutions that can be discovered.

## Care

It can be taken for granted that any form of counselling or psycho-therapy needs to be conducted with reference to a set of ethical principles. A key facet of the role of professional associations and government regulatory bodies is to ensure that practitioners acquire knowledge and decision-making skills around ethical issues during their training, and remain informed about ethical issues over the course of their careers, and that procedures are available for clients and service users to complain about ethical misconduct. These systems are predominantly guided by principles and values that are considered to be universal moral truths that apply to any professional activity. They exist to ensure that bad things do not happen to people.

While acknowledging the importance of principle-based ethics, and adhering to relevant professional ethical codes, pluralistic therapy goes further in embedding ethical awareness into the actual practice of therapy. In doing this, pluralistic therapy draws on developments in what has become known as *relational ethics* (Gabriel and Casemore, 2009). Rather than seeking ethical guidance from universal and impartial general principles, relational ethics seeks to ground the ethical process in the relational commitment of persons to each other, in ways that take account of the context or environment in which therapy is conducted. Relational ethics pays active attention to the feelings and emotions of those who are involved, their cultural beliefs and values and the question of how mutual respect can be maintained. The aim is to create an 'ethical space' within which the practitioner and the service user can feel as free as possible to engage as fully as possible in a therapeutic process. This endeavour can be regarded as a form of 'positive' ethics, because it aims to make a positive contribution to the quality of the work that is being done, in addition to avoiding harm. In prioritising the relationship between therapist and client, relational ethics is consistent with the type of ethical stance adopted by many experienced and effective therapists (Jennings et al., 2005).

A key idea in relational ethics is that that of respecting the 'otherness of the Other'. The existential philosopher Emmanuel Levinas argued that this kind of moral stance is primary in human interaction and represents a form of understanding that is more basic than cognitive or theoretical sense-making. It is a profound and highly challenging position to adopt, because it involves an acceptance that authentic interaction with another person (i.e. not treating them as an 'object' or a 'case' or assuming that they are the 'same') involves recognising and affirming the ways in which that person is unique, active and reflective, and different from oneself (Sayre, 2005; Whiting, Nebeker and Fife, 2005). This is not an easy thing to accomplish as a therapist when one has been trained to diagnose clients or interpret their actions and problems in terms of relevant theory and research. In pluralistic therapy, this ethical stance is reflected in the expectation that the therapist will be open to learning from the client. It is also reflected in the willingness of the therapist to be known (e.g. to share their ideas) and to engage in dialogue around the differences between the point of view of the client and that of the therapist – these are practices of mutuality that invite the client to authentically experience the therapist as an 'other'.

In pluralistic therapy, there is a great deal of emphasis on explaining options, checking out with the client whether they feel that what is happening in therapy is helpful and eliciting client suggestions (Cooper and McLeod, 2011). These activities represent a conscious intention to embed informed consent into the moment-by-moment process of therapy. Although informed consent is a central element in principle-based ethics, it is not always implemented in therapy practice (O'Neill, 1998). There are, in fact, serious difficulties around obtaining informed consent at the start of treatment, because it is hard to provide the client with relevant information about what might happen in therapy. It may also be hard for the client to take this information on board if they are in a state of emotional crisis. By contrast, adopting a style of process consent, which takes place in the context of a deepening relationship and unfolding process of change, helps to create a space in which the client feels safe, respected and in control.

A further dimension of relational ethics arises from an appreciation that the client is not merely an autonomous self-contained individual, but also a member of a society that is characterised by injustice, oppression, exploitation and cruelty. As a result, effective and respectful therapy may involve naming and confronting sources of oppression. This aspect of therapeutic work has been described in recent years as a *social justice* orientation (Goodman et al., 2004). This stance may involve such activities as supporting a client, where relevant, to engage with groups that are active in opposing oppressive activities such as bullying, sexual violence, racism and exclusion of those with disabilities, and finding ways to actively fight back in the sense of helping to make the world a better place. A distinctive feature of pluralistic practice is a willingness to engage in dialogue around social issues and political action.

A crucial aspect of relational ethics is that it highlights the significance of the concept of *care*. Following Lynch (2007, p. 551), this stance emphasises 'the importance of other-centred work arising from our interdependencies and dependencies as affective, relational beings . . . [and] the centrality of *caring* for the preservation and self-actualisation of the human species'. Caring becomes not merely an unpaid or low-paid form of work carried out by those at the bottom of the social hierarchy, but is regarded as part of the ethical responsibility that all of us hold towards each other and to the planet. An appreciation of relational ethics, therefore, leads pluralistic therapists to develop a language and consciousness of the centrality of care in their work with clients. At its root, this involves a willingness to say that you care, and to question any signs of absence of care.

Conceptually, by incorporating relational ethics in the way that it does, pluralistic therapy introduces a different set of criteria to the task of deciding whether therapy has been effective. On the whole, therapy is considered to have been successful if the client has achieved their goals, or is satisfied with what they have gained, or reports a lessening of troubling symptoms. Occasionally, therapy can go beyond this, and be experienced as transformative. Some-times, therapy can be unhelpful or even damaging for the client. From a pluralistic standpoint that invites consideration of multiple perspectives, all of these perspectives are relevant and important. However, relational ethics suggests a further way of assessing the value of therapy – has there been a full and genuine engagement of two (or more) participants in a process of working together in an honest, constructive and respectful manner? Many clients are well aware that the issues that they bring to therapy are intractable at that point in their life. For such individuals, knowledge that their therapist has given it his or her best shot, gone the extra mile, has offered a space in which they could make a similar effort and has genuinely cared, is evidence of good therapy.

7

# Evidence

The development of pluralistic therapy has taken place at a time when governments, health organisations and increasingly, clients, have highlighted the importance of the principle of evidence-based practice (EBP): the requirement that therapy should be informed by the best research evidence that is currently available. For the most part, EBP guidelines have been dominated by a tendency to favour empirically validated therapies that are supported by evidence from randomised controlled/clinical trials (RCTs). From a pluralistic perspective, although RCT evidence is undoubtedly valuable, it represents only one among many sources of potentially relevant research evidence. Pluralistic evidence-based practice therefore goes beyond traditional models of EBP in four main ways: (1) questioning the validity of a hierarchy of evidence and replacing it with an 'evidence-network' stance which acknowledges the strengths and limitations of all sources of evidence; (2) offering particular support to sources of evidence, such as qualitative studies, that seek to document the views of clients; (3) recognition of the value of evidence generated within individual cases (e.g. arising from client feedback measures), particularly when grounded in criteria identified by the client; and (4) adoption of a critical perspective that takes account of political influences on the creation and dissemination of scientific knowledge.

A crucial aspect of a pluralistic stance in relation to EBP is that its focus is not on general truths (e.g. the relative effectiveness of different approaches to therapy) but on what makes a difference to a particular client at a particular point in time. Many therapy researchers pay homage to the influential statement made by Paul (1967, p. 44), that therapy research should strive to arrive at generalizable conclusions around 'what treatment, by whom, is most effective for this individual with that specific problem, and under what set of circumstances?' In pluralistic therapy, this position can be reframed more directly, from the client's perspective, as 'what works for *me*?'

At the present time, and for many years, the field of psychotherapy research has been highly productive, generating many thousands of studies. This situation makes it possible to search for studies that contribute to developing a better understanding of what *could* be helpful for a client at a specific point in therapy. It is unlikely that there will be evidence from randomised trials that can be directly mapped onto the needs of the client, because such studies are more oriented towards broad-brush questions about the relative efficacy of different interventions than towards informing decision-making during the process of working with a client. The kinds of research evidence that are more likely to produce relevant insights are qualitative interview-based studies that capture the client's experience of overcoming a particular type of problem, professional knowledge studies that document therapist learning and wisdom around specific areas of work and detailed case studies that describe how the process of therapy can unfold in different ways (McLeod, 2016). An example of the kind of evidence base that can be invaluable for therapists is the body of qualitative research that exists around the experience of depression and recovery from depression (e.g. Chambers et al., 2015; Oliffe et al., 2012; Rhodes and Smith, 2010; Ridge and Ziebland, 2012; Wilson and Giddings, 2010). These studies allow the reader to see beyond psychological and psychiatric theories and assumptions, and gain insight into what it is actually like to overcome this problem.

While research evidence is undoubtedly valuable as a source of knowledge for practice, a pluralistic perspective invites consideration of the relevance of other ways of knowing. For example, both the client and therapist have access to massive reservoirs of personal knowledge around dealing with relationships, managing emotions and learning from experience. They are also able to draw on personal, common-sense or formal theories. Pluralistic therapists develop a capacity to move backward and forward between different ways of knowing. For example, a therapist working with a client who has a marriage problem may know, from their own personal experience, that it is helpful to understand how early attachment patterns are played out in spousal relationships. The therapist may also know that there is good evidence that cognitive-behavioural problem-solving interventions have been shown to be helpful for such clients. Acknowledging and staying with the tension between these two sources of knowledge and evidence allows the therapist to arrive at a differentiated way of understanding what might possibly be most useful in that particular case. It may be possible to identify specific aspects of the client's difficulties that reflect attachment processes, and other aspects that may be responsive to a problem-solving approach.

There is a strong emphasis in pluralistic therapy on working collaboratively – finding ways to harness the strengths and insights of both the therapist and client. This principle extends to the domain of research-informed practice. It is important to regard the client as an active researcher into their own condition. The client makes observations, reads things, develops their own theory of what is wrong and how it can be sorted and tests hypotheses. The client also investigates the process of therapy and has ideas about what has been helpful (or not) in the therapy hour. It can be useful to initiate conversations around these issues. Some clients may be interested in the research evidence that informs the approach taken by their therapist, and may even want to read research studies. Some clients may want to know about the general success rates for psychotherapy for a particular condition, or the average number of sessions attended by clients with that problem.

8

# Design

Historically, counselling and psychotherapy have been primarily understood as applied disciplines with their roots in psychology. From this perspective, the activities undertaken by therapists have been viewed as *interventions*. Pluralism invites and encourages consideration of multiple ways of knowing. This has resulted in an appreciation of the possibilities associated with thinking about the similarities between therapy and art. From an art perspective, what therapists and clients do together can be viewed as a type of *making* (Gauntlett, 2011): making a meaningful experience within the therapy hour, making a new life, re-making oneself. The client and the therapist make, build or construct something together.

An art-informed perspective opens up a number of ways to make sense of the identity of being a therapist. A therapist can be regarded as, in part, a craftsperson who possesses a high degree of skill in making a particular type of product (Sennett, 2008). A craftsperson belongs to a craft community, has a workshop space of some kind and has at some point been an apprentice to a 'master'. A therapist may also be viewed as being, in some respects, like an artist. As with artists, therapists express themselves through their work. A therapy session may be viewed as kind of performance art.

The concept of *design* has a special resonance and relevance for pluralistic therapy. Rather than merely seeking to create a specific type of predefined therapeutic experience or product, the therapist and client search through the many possibilities that are available to them, and combine known elements in a combination that is the best fit with the goals and preferences of the client. It can be helpful to envisage client and therapist as co-participants in what has been described by Brown (2009) as comprising the following stages:

- Creating a space where mistakes can be made;
- Observing everyday life, both to gain a sense of the creative possibilities that exist within it, and how it might be rearranged to produce greater life satisfaction;
- Generating ideas and possibilities, often using a collaborative team approach;
- Dealing with complexity through visual thinking and storytelling; and
- Prototyping: learning what works by testing possible solutions ('fail early, fail often').

Brown (2009) points out that the product that emerges from a design process can not only be a physical object, such as an iPhone, but can also take the form of a service, such as patient-centred health care, or a virtual space such as a website. From a design perspective, the quality of the final product can be evaluated along two dimensions (Norman, 2002). First, the product needs to be usable, in terms of fulfilling a function in everyday life, and to accomplish this in a way that is seamless or efficient, otherwise potential users will just drop it. Second, the product needs to be aesthetically pleasing, so that the user develops an emotional attachment to it and feels pleasure when using it.

These ideas provide a valuable way to think about what happens in pluralistic therapy; the idea of therapy as design is revisited at various places in the present book. Pluralistic therapy can be seen as a process of both designing a therapy experience and re-designing some aspect of the client's life. The client and therapist each have different, but equally vital roles to play in the design process. Most therapies concentrate primarily on the implementation of procedures that are already defined. By contrast, pluralistic therapy seeks to create new combinations and adaptations of existing procedures, alongside any other ideas that are culturally available to the client and therapist. Observing the characteristics of well-designed objects and services that we encounter in our lives, and learning about how artists and designers think and work (Gompertz, 2015), represent important sources of learning and inspiration for pluralistic therapists.

The use of cultural resources is a distinctive and significant aspect of pluralistic practice (see Chapter 25). A cultural resource is any activity that can function as a way of coping with stress, an arena for sustaining supportive relationships and a source of meaning, well-being and pleasure. There are many different types of cultural resources that can be relevant for clients, and the process of recognising and re-activating the client's resources can be a highly satisfying and productive aspect of pluralistic work. Pluralistic therapy aims to assist the client to re-design or re-build their personal niche (Willi, 1999; Willi, Frei and Gunther, 2000) so that it works better (i.e. the person is moving forward in the direction of achieving what they want to get out of their life) and, ideally, so that it is more pleasing. Some cultural resources function to keep life moving in the right direction. For example, someone with a stressful job might have a rule to walk their dog every evening as a means of creating a tangible boundary between work and home. Other cultural resources, such as spiritual experience and art, may function as a means of incorporating spaces into the everyday life of the person that operate as touchstones or reminders of transcendent and aesthetic aspects of being human (De Botton and Armstrong, 2013).

9

## Purpose

An explicit focus on client *purpose* and *agency* informs the practice of pluralistic therapy. A capacity for intentionality, purposefulness and future orientation is intrinsic to being human. The notion of the 'good life' as an ideal towards which the person actively strives represents an important way in which personal and cultural values are expressed.

The significance of client agency reflects an important underlying theme in counselling and psychotherapy theory and practice. Classic perspectives on this topic include Bandura's self-efficacy theory, Schafer's psychoanalytic 'action language', existential theory around intentionality, Glasser's choice theory, the concept of positioning in postmodern therapies and various strengths-based and solution-oriented approaches to therapy. The concept of the 'active' or agential client is discussed in detail in Bohart and Tallman (2001) and Bohart (2006). The micro-processes through which client agency is expressed in therapy have been documented in several studies, for example Dundas et al. (2009), Gibson and Cartwright (2013), Glasman, Finlay and Brock (2004), Hoener et al. (2012) and Lowe and Murray (2014). The ways in which therapists encourage client agency have been explored by Oddli and Rønnestad (2012).

Pluralistic therapy activities such as metacommunication, collaboration and shared decision-making around tasks and methods, and responsiveness to client preferences and cultural resources, have the aim of positioning the client as actively striving to make meaning and fulfil personal life goals that express core values. Collaborative case formulation and the identification of therapy goals are ways in which the client's sense of a future are highlighted, made visible and documented within pluralistic therapy.

In addition to purpose-oriented and future-oriented procedures, the promotion of client agency is expressed in sensitivity to language. Different ways of talking about self imply either an agentic or non-agentic stance. For instance, it is possible to view oneself from the outside, as an object. This stance is typically accompanied by the use of general attributions such as being 'extravert' or 'tall'. By contrast, it is possible to view self or other as an agent or author of their experience, through telling stories that account for how one acted in a particular situation. Although both perspectives coexist in everyday life and in therapy discourse, an agentic stance in relation to personal experience offers more leverage in terms of learning and change. A valuable discussion of the interplay between these perspectives can be found in McAdams (2013), whose approach is consistent with pluralism in reflecting a 'both/and' strategy for making sense of complex issues.

Different types of conversation can contribute to client learning that is related to the expression of agency and purpose. For example, it may be helpful to invite a person to reflect on how they channel their attention and purposeful action, or even to offer feedback from an external observer perspective on what the person appears to be doing. A client might come to realise through such conversations that he 'depresses' himself by repeatedly reminding himself of his failures, and avoiding looking at other people (thus not allowing himself to pick up cues around their interest in what he had to say). A further agency-focused conversational strategy is associated with inviting the person to be aware of how he or she talks about an issue. In its simplest form, this method may involve commenting that the person is talking in the second or third person, or in abstract terms ('depression makes you want to hide away from people') and inviting them to try saying the same thing in a more direct way ('when I feel sad, I want to hide from people').

A different type of agency-oriented intervention is to encourage clients to pay attention to events and episodes in their lives where their actions have led to preferred outcomes. This can enable a person to become more able to accept that they do have a capacity to take responsibility and make changes. Within pluralistic therapeutic practice, each time the therapist facilitates a discussion of options around which tasks are most important, or which methods might be most helpful in progressing these tasks, they are conversationally positioning the client as someone who is able to make choices and initiate action.

Viewing the client as active and intentional makes it possible to recognise the potential risks in using diagnostic labels that attribute the person's difficulties to processes that are non-agentic. Although no longer promoted by the psychiatric research community, the notion of depression as arising from a chemical imbalance in the brain has become a familiar way of thinking for many people. The risk here is that such a perspective is self-limiting in the sense of reducing purposeful action to the mere act of taking medication once a day. A pluralistic approach to therapy encourages conversations that allow meaning bridges to be constructed between the position of seeing oneself as biochemically faulty and seeing oneself as possessing the power to change things. There is evidence that many people construct such meaning bridges on their own initiative. In a study of experiences of women in New Zealand around taking antidepressant medication, Cartwright, Gibson and Read (2016) found that many of them used the effect of the medication to 'kick-start' new initiatives around ways of coping and relating to others.

10

# Collaboration

The concept of collaboration represents a cornerstone of pluralistic practice, which is discussed in several places in the present book. The notion of collaboration is also widely discussed in the therapy literature as a whole (Lambert and Cattani, 2012), for example in relation to the idea of collaborative empiricism in cognitive behavioural therapy (CBT) or as an aspect of the therapeutic alliance (Tryon and Winograd, 2011). A pluralistic understanding of collaboration builds on these existing perspectives, but takes them further. Mainstream therapy theories tend to define collaboration as a process in which the therapist provides the ideas, intervention and structure, and the client works with them to ensure that these strategies are effectively applied in the context of their individual life circumstances. By contrast, in pluralistic therapy both the client and the therapist contribute ideas, intervention and structure. This means that collaboration in pluralistic therapy takes a greater significance, in carrying the weight of the therapy process. Anderson (1996) has described this as a 'partnership' rather than a 'complying-with' philosophy of practice.

Collaboration in pluralistic therapy comprises a set of key elements: turn-taking, sensitivity to language, putting difference to work and responsiveness. Turn-taking is important because it establishes a rhythm and structure to therapy conversation that makes it possible for each participant to have openings where they can contribute their ideas, and also times when they can be receptive to the ideas of the other person (Sundet et al., 2016). Awkwardness in turn-taking, for example when one participant is silenced, or there is a lot of talking over the other, may mean that there are difficulties in collaboration. Sensitivity to language is essential because there are many subtle ways in which either party may pretend to be engaged in collaboration but are in fact avoiding engaging fully with the other. For example, while therapists may appear on the face of it to be listening and reflecting back in a way that seems to be all about empowering the client, a closer examination of what they are actually saying may disclose that their word choices are reformulating the client's experience to conform to the therapist's theory (Anderson, 1996; Strong, 2000). Putting difference to work (Sundet et al., 2016) reflects the fact that client and therapist have different things to offer, arising from different life experiences. Effectively working together, in therapy as in any other area of life, is not usually a matter of both people doing the same thing, but involves dovetailing the talents of one with the skills of the other. Finally, responsiveness refers to the ability of the therapist to align themselves with the intentions, sense of direction and relational style of the client (Kramer and Stiles, 2015; Stiles, Honos-Webb and Surko, 1998). Lack of therapist responsiveness means that client ideas and initiatives get lost and do not enter the mix. If this goes on for long enough, it is likely that the client will lose interest, and stop trying to influence what is happening.

Apart from functioning as a means of ensuring that the most appropriate methods and interventions are brought to bear on the client's goals, collaboration may have a deeper meaning for some clients:

> Collaboration in relation to goals and tasks in therapy is an implicit acknowledgement of clients' directedness toward the future, the client's sense of self-worth, the client's isolation, relatedness, and freedom, the client's agency, and the changing nature of the client and the world . . . improved outcome in therapy that emphasizes goal consensus and collaboration is partly because of the fact that the client is confronted with a range of existential conditions.
>
> (Mackrill, 2010, p. 104)

The point here is that while doing collaboration may have certain therapeutic effects (e.g. implementing effective change methods), the experience of reflecting on collaboration (e.g. when it has been hard, or after a successful collaborative episode) can have an additional therapeutic value, as a gateway into meaning-making conversations that touch on issues of identity and responsibility (Wong, 2012).

In pluralistic therapy, the concept of collaboration is used to refer to the routine and pragmatic effort to listen, to acknowledge the ideas of the other person and to arrive at a plan of action (Tryon, 2013). This activity is linked, in ways that are hard to define, to the experience of dialogue. The experience of dialogue is intrinsically satisfying, energising, meaningful, memorable and healing, and occurs when each person is open to the other, and to their self, in a way that flows and leads to the emergence of new insights. A pluralistic conceptualisation of dialogue is the topic for the next chapter.

11

# Dialogue

Much of the preliminary work of pluralistic therapy (e.g. building a capacity for collaboration, use of feedback, conversations around goals, tasks and methods) has the aim of creating the possibility of dialogue. Dialogue may be considered a helpful and healing experience in itself. The sharing of ideas that occurs in open dialogue helps to generate new problem solutions and strategies. Engaging in authentic dialogue involves an affirmation of being accepted as a person. It is energising. It is also a valuable life skill that is essential for interpersonal intimacy in everyday relationships.

In order to facilitate dialogue, it is important to be able to differentiate between dialogue and other forms of linguistic interaction. For example, instruction is a type of conversation in which one person tells the other what to do, and observes whether their directions are being followed. Monologue refers to situations in which one person speaks without leaving space for the other to respond, or where the other is being relatively quiet or passive. In a discussion, both people speak but engage in information exchange without necessarily disclosing their own personal stance. In a debate, each person speaks from their own personal stance, with the intention of proving the other person to be wrong; listening takes place but only to collect information that can be argued as being in error.

By contrast, dialogical conversation encompasses a set of unique features. Each person speaks from his or her own stance or position on the topic. Each person tries to understand and accept the position of the other. Statements refer back to previous utterances and reach forward to a further response from the other. There is some reference to conceptual or metaphoric meaning (i.e. not merely an exchange of factual information). No one person controls or dominates the interaction. There is a sustained thread of exploration of a specific topic. There is the possibility of learning – a 'fusion of horizons' in which some kind of new understanding emerges from the two perspectives.

Dialogue can be understood as a form of purposeful talk that includes opportunities for the full expression of different 'voices', 'selves' or positions. There is close listening to the explicit and implicit meaning being expressed by the other. There is a commitment to respect, take account of and make sense of the point of view of the 'other'. The conversation is characterised by turn-taking and responsiveness.

Conventionally, the process of therapy can be viewed as primarily constructed around two modes of conversation. The therapist may adopt a listening, empathic stance, intended to enable the client to tell their story in a manner that deepens its meaningfulness and experiential depth. Alternatively, a therapist may engage in a form of instructional, psycho-educational or information-giving talk, for instance when introducing a task or exercise, or pointing out that the session is nearing its close. Dialogue represents a further mode of therapeutic conversation, one that requires the therapist to express his or her personal response to the client. It opens up a situation in which both participants become respectfully aware of differences in their positions, which can then lead, if the conversation is sustained, to the creation of a point of connection or 'meaning bridge' that allows common ground to be identified across the two positions. The existence of this new idea takes each participant further than their initial starting point. Dialogue typically facilitates learning on the part of the therapist as well as the client.

It can be hard for pluralistic therapists to grasp the significance of dialogue. Western culture provides few models of good dialogue, and in fact provides innumerable examples of 'anti-dialogue' in settings such as parliamentary debates, student–teacher interactions in schools and the way that people talk to each other in hierarchical command structures such as the military. It can be helpful to learn from examples of constructive dialogue in other cultural settings, such as the Commission for Truth and Justice in South Africa, and ancient cultural traditions such as *hui* (New Zealand) and *palaver* (Africa).

It is also useful to be aware of the ways in which dialogue is grounded in non-verbal or embodied interaction. Research by Colwyn Trevarthen and others has analysed the 'dance' and musicality of mother–infant interaction as a form of dialogue: the mother follows the baby, then adds something (Malloch and Trevarthen, 2010). Emotional expression and attunement, bodily synchrony, pacing, voice quality and proxemics are important factors in dialogue.

Studies by Steen Halling and his colleagues have identified some of the features of relationships in which dialogue is most likely to occur. These include *structure* (disciplined focus on ultimate goals), *freedom* (the capacity to be playful and imaginative) and *trust* (being open and receptive to what is new in the other person's experience) (Halling, Kunz and Rowe, 1994; Halling, Leifer and Rowe, 2006). Valuable accounts of how these qualities are exhibited in dialogical conversations in therapy can be found in Seikkula (2011) and Schmid (2001).

12

# Preference

Over the last decade, a great deal of evidence has accumulated, from a wide range of research studies, that clients are aware of what might be helpful for them and what they need to do in therapy, and that therapy is more effective when it takes account of such preferences. The emergence of client preferences as a significant factor in predicting therapy outcomes would appear to result from sociocultural changes, such as the increasing proportion of the population that has studied psychology or has participated in therapy, and the widespread access to information about therapy through the internet. Mainstream approaches to therapy, such as psychodynamic and cognitive behavioural therapy (CBT), developed at a time when the influence of client preferences was less significant or was not understood. Because it has emerged at a time when evidence of preference effects had started to be known, pluralistic therapy has been able to incorporate this phenomenon as a central element of its practice. The evidence from research suggests that client preferences do not easily map onto models of therapy. For example the preferences of some clients may make them a good fit for a mainstream purist model of therapy such as CBT. However, the majority of clients appear to express 'mix and match' preferences that include ideas and interventions from different models.

In order to take account of client preferences, it is necessary to appreciate their complexity, and also the issues and difficulties associated with the expression of preferences in therapy settings. The meaning of 'preference' is itself multifaceted. The concept of preferences overlaps with other related constructs such as expectations, attitudes, beliefs, theory of change, theory of cure and hope. In some circumstances, these alternative terms may make more sense to clients. The specific aspect of the concept of preference that differs from these other ideas is that it implies action. For example a client may state that they expect their therapist to challenge them, but in itself this does not mean that they actually favour this kind of behaviour – they just happen to believe that it is one of the things that therapists do. By contrast, if a client indicates a preference for their therapist to challenge them, it suggests that they believe that such behaviour will be beneficial, and that they will be likely to respond constructively to it.

Another aspect of the complexity of preferences relates to the extent to which a client is consciously aware of what they believe will be helpful. It may be that a client is in a position to say that 'silence is not helpful for me – I just freeze and get embarrassed.' Alternatively, it may be that a preference is implicit or out of immediate awareness, and it is only when something happens (e.g. silence) that a client realises that it is not helpful for them. Preferences may be nuanced and conditional:

Silence is useful if I realise that it is a space for reflection and there is no expectation for me to speak, but is not useful if it makes me feel stupid and inadequate because my therapist is waiting for me to say something intelligent.

Preferences may be strongly held, or a matter of relative indifference. Positive preferences refer to activities or characteristics of therapy that are seen to be facilitative. Negative preferences are experiences that the client believes would lead them to quit therapy, or be harmful.

Studies of client preferences indicate that there are many potential choice-points that are relevant for clients. At the broadest level, there are some people who believe that therapy is valuable, and others who believe it is worthless and would never want to see a therapist. There are also strong preferences for and against medication such as antidepressants. There is also evidence for preference around therapy approaches, such as CBT and psychodynamic therapy. However, there is stronger evidence linking preferences to specific therapeutic activities (expressing emotion, behaviour change, receiving support, etc.) and therapist relational style. Preferences have also been recorded in relation to the age, gender, ethnicity, sexual orientation and apparel of therapists, and to a wide range of practical arrangements such as timing, location and length of therapy. It is clear that it would be very hard, in practical terms, to engage a client in discussion around all of these preferences, and it would be impossible to fulfil all of them. Within pluralistic therapy, the intention is to engage in sufficient exploration of preferences to the point at which the client is comfortable with what is on offer, or realises that what they really want or need is not available, and that a different type of help would be more suitable for them.

Typically, clients do not enter therapy with a clearly articulated list of preferences. Some clients may be reluctant to talk about their preferences, for fear of being judged as stupid by their therapist. In general, clients and therapists tend to work under time pressure, and are not interested in holding extended discussions around preferences. For these reasons, many pluralistic therapists make use of brief questionnaire forms that invite clients to indicate their preferences for particular therapy activities or therapist behaviours and qualities. Alternatively, a brief focused interview, for example during initial assessment, can be highly effective in eliciting not only client preferences but also the reasons behind these preferences (Vollmer et al., 2009; Walls, McLeod and McLeod, 2016).

Within the process of therapy, genuine therapist curiosity around client preferences, and sensitive responsiveness to client expression of preferences, is seen as contributing to the construction of a positive, collaborative working relationship, as well as positioning the client as someone whose views are worthy of consideration. Conversations around preferences, and responsiveness to what emerges in these conversations, can also be regarded as a key part of the ethical necessity to obtain informed consent for treatment (O'Neill, 1998). As with other ethical procedures, when the client perceives their therapist to be acting in a professional and respectful manner, they are more likely to commit themselves to therapy in an active fashion.

13

# Deciding

Pluralistic therapy is based on an assumption that shared decision-making between client and therapist is an important factor in the process of effective therapy. Shared decision-making may refer to global or overarching aspects of therapy, such as goals to be pursued, the general strategy to be adopted or the timing, location and number of sessions. It can also refer to moment-by-moment choice points within therapy sessions (e.g. deciding how much time to devote to each task or topic, deciding that a particular issue has been resolved or deciding how best to explore an issue).

The concept of shared decision-making has received substantial attention in health care. In many situations, a medical diagnosis may lead to a range of different treatment possibilities. For example, back pain may be treated by medication, surgery, physiotherapy, lifestyle advice, yoga or watchful waiting. In addition, some patients may be influenced by indigenous health beliefs and remedies, such as feng shui, that do not correspond to contemporary medical theory and research. There is considerable evidence that patients do not adhere to treatment regimens that do not match their beliefs and preferences, leading to a waste of resources and exacerbation of their condition (Mulley, Trimble and Elwyn, 2012). As a result, there has been a substantial amount of research and practice development within medicine and health care around the ways in which doctors (or nurses and other healthcare practitioners) can engage in shared decision-making that leads to mutually acceptable interventions (Legare and Thompson-Leduc, 2014; Shay and Lafata, 2015). Shared decision-making protocols typically incorporate the following steps:

1    The professional informs the patient that a decision is to be made and that the patient's opinion is important.

2    The professional explains the options and the pros and cons of
     each relevant option.
3    The professional and patient discuss the patient's preferences;
     the professional supports the patient in deliberation.
4    The professional and patient discuss the patient's decisional
     role preference, make or defer the decision and discuss possible
     follow-up.

(Stiggelbout, Pieterse and De Haes, 2015, p. 1173)

The development and use of decision tools, which provide information for patients, has provided health care workers with a structure
from which to organise effective conversations with patients around
shared decision-making.

There are several ways in which shared decision-making in psychotherapy differs from shared decision-making in medicine. In medicine,
it is generally clear that some kind of decision needs to be made – the
aim of the conversation between the doctor/nurse and the patient is
to agree on which is the best among several options. By contrast, in
psychotherapy the conversation may be oriented towards arriving at a
point at which a decision can be made at all: deciding to stop misusing
drugs, deciding to have a child, deciding to leave a marriage or deciding whether to keep living. For many clients, the actual act of making
a decision may be the most important thing that they do in therapy.
Building a track record of working together to make decisions around
the small details of therapy, such as what to talk about today, or whether
to meet weekly, creates a decision-making framework within which big
life decisions can be explored when the time comes.

Beyond these primary outcomes, there are some other, less obvious ways that shared decision-making may facilitate constructive
learning and change. For some clients, acquiring practical knowledge and skills around what it is like to participate in shared decision-
making may be highly relevant to everyday situations in work and
family life that have been characterised by an inability to arrive at
agreed ways of dealing with issues. A focus on deciding together can
also have the effect of opening up a space for exploring what it means
to make a choice or decision, or what it means to be in a relationship

in which one is allowed to decide, or is open to hearing and accepting the ideas of another person.

The concept of shared decision-making functions as a counter-balance to the common misunderstanding that pluralistic practice involves slavishly following what the client wants. This is not the case. While following the client is a sound guiding principle, the aim is to ensure the fullest exploration of all possibilities, drawing on ideas and suggestions from *both* client *and* therapist. It may be that, through such a discussion, the client comes to see that the suggestions of their therapist make sense to them, and represent a more viable direction than their own ideas.

14

# Method

In pluralistic therapy, a *method* refers to a sequence of joint action that is carried out with the intention of contributing to the achievement of a therapeutic task. The concept of method is similar to other terms used in the psychotherapy literature such as 'technique', 'intervention' and 'procedure'. Compared to the other terms, the idea of a 'method' differs in two main respects. First, there is no assumption that what is done necessarily arises from the professional training, skills and knowledge of the therapist. Instead, a 'method' may be suggested by the client, or by the therapist and client devising something together. Second, method refers to any action that makes a difference. It can therefore refer to micro-actions, such as agreeing that it would be helpful for the therapist to ask more questions at a particular moment in therapy, through to longer sequences such as a planned sequence of behaviour change including homework assignments that can span several sessions.

In order to facilitate collaboration around methods, a therapist needs to be able to initiate conversations with the client around this topic. This requires an awareness of suitable opportunities for engaging in such conversations and an appreciation of what it is that needs to be discussed. Pluralistic therapy is informed by client goals, which are then broken down into a series of sub-goals, or tasks, that need to be accomplished in order to attain the goal. The therapist and client then explore and agree on the best method (or combination of methods) to complete the task.

It is never too early to express curiosity about the client's views about which methods might work best for them. For example, the client may have ideas about what worked or did not work in relation to previous therapy or informal help they have experienced. It is also likely that they may have privately tried out different methods on their own initiative.

To talk about methods, it is necessary to be able to draw on ideas about possible causal sequences. For example if a client wants to control panic attacks, it is helpful if the therapist is able to conceptualise this issue in terms of a possible sequence of client actions and responses that link anticipatory thoughts, breathing, bodily states, catastrophic thinking about consequences, withdrawal from social support and so on. When discussing potential change methods, it may be useful to talk the client through such a sequence or model, leading to a stage of shared decision-making around what the client might do to break the chain, through either eliminating an existing action/response or introducing a new one. To be able to facilitate such conversations, the therapist needs to be able to translate ideas from theory, research and practical/personal experience into sequential, script-like formulations.

It is unlikely that the actual word 'method' would be used when talking with a client. Being a competent pluralistic therapist involves talking about methods using language that makes sense to the client. Sometimes this can involve merely directly referring to the matter in hand: 'it might be useful for us to talk about what you could do to manage these awful feelings of anxiety, or even to move on from them completely . . . do you have any thoughts?' At other times, a client and therapist may develop their own language: 'I remember when you described how you overcame your fear before, you talked about "being a giant" . . . can you tell me a bit more about how that worked?' In addition to the attainment of tasks and goals, conversations around method choice are viewed as instilling hope and encouraging client reflection.

Methods may have their origins in a wide range of sources. Models of therapy, and in particular treatment manuals, represent a rich source of techniques/methods for facilitating change. Other methods may found in cultural traditions and practices familiar to the client and therapist (Mahrer, 2007). Yet other methods may be idiosyncratic, arising from the personal life experience of the client or therapist.

With respect to methods that have been formally identified within the therapy literature, a pluralistic perspective holds that these activities are regarded as capable of being disembedded from theoretical approaches. For example, it is possible to work with irrational beliefs without incorporating other elements of Rational Emotive Behaviour Therapy, or work with dreams without applying psychodynamic or Gestalt therapy ways of making sense of this intervention. While certain combinations of concepts and methods have been bundled together by psychotherapists as constituting coherent models or approaches, at the level of the individual client these therapy 'packages' are unlikely to have much meaning. Instead, clients are more interested in pragmatic strategies for dealing with immediate issues. In addition, clients are likely to draw on a wide array of ideas that they have come across over the course of their lives regarding how to make sense of problems in living. A trained therapist may believe that methods that focus on changing irrational beliefs form part of the therapy process that assumes that client difficulties are primarily cognitive in nature. However, a client may believe that their difficulties arise from family issues or early trauma, and still find it helpful to learn how to stop undermining themselves through irrational thought processes.

In pluralistic therapy, the methods used by the therapist are based in mastery of core counselling skills, such as listening, using different types of questions, reflecting meaning, challenging and so on (Cooper, 2016; McLeod and McLeod, 2011). Counselling skills are basic facilitation tools that can be flexibly adapted and improvised to serve a variety of functions.

A pluralistic therapist invites metacommunication and shared decision-making around the choice of methods, and reflection on the effectiveness of methods. A method that has not contributed to desired change can be viewed as an opportunity for learning: 'How could we have approached that in a better way? Is there another approach we might be taking?' For some clients, there may be significant learning arising from the realisation that social interaction, or any goal-directed activity, rarely proceeds in a straightforward, linear, scripted manner, and that the capacity to improvise and make adjustments is a key life skill. There are other therapeutic 'by-products' that may be associated with a pluralistic focus on methods. Being invited and encouraged by their therapist to talk about methods ('what is helpful for me, and what is not') opens up possibilities for reflective functioning, which is likely to be a helpful therapeutic process in its own right. Working together on the selection, modification and evaluation of change methods represents a form of joint action between therapist and client, which can help to build a collaborative relationship. It can also build hope, through the implication that many possibilities exist and that sooner or later the one that works for them will be found.

15

# Understanding

In a review of studies in which clients, who had participated in a wide range of different types of therapy, described what had been helpful for them, Timulak (2007) found that increased insight and self-understanding was one of the factors that was mentioned most often, and that feeling understood by their therapist had been particularly valuable for them. These findings are not surprising. People seek formal therapeutic help when they are confused or 'at a loss' about making sense of what is happening in their relationships and in their inner emotional life and thoughts. It seems clear that a large number of people also actively try to understand their problems through reading self-help books and websites, and studying psychology, as well as through non-psychological sources such as religion and philosophy. The acquisition of new understanding, often described as 'insight', can be regarded as a common factor across all approaches to therapy (Castonguay and Hill, 2007). Theories of therapy can be viewed as stories or narratives that function as tools for understanding that give sense and meaning to the challenges faced by individuals in their lives (Hansen, 2006).

In pluralistic therapy, the wish to gain perspective or understanding in relation to life difficulties is regarded as a therapeutic task that arises to a greater or lesser extent in most cases. This kind of therapeutic activity can take a variety of forms. In some instances, the client may arrive at their own understanding or insight, as an outcome of talking about an issue, or engaging in reflection. Sometimes the client may be helped to apply ways of making sense that are already available to them, to a situation that is hard to understand. In some cases, the therapist may teach the client about certain ways of making sense, or suggest sources where such knowledge is available.

The development of understanding may be narrowly focused, as in learning about the fight-flight response, or broader in scope, as in making connections between personal experience and broader meaning systems from religion and politics (Wong, 2012).

Making progress in pluralistic therapy depends on the establishment of a sufficient degree of shared understanding between client and therapist regarding goals, tasks and methods. In pluralistic therapy, shared understanding is not taken to mean that the client and the therapist necessarily always share the same point of view. Differences between the client and therapist, for example around the importance of a specific therapy goal, are regarded as opportunities for productive dialogue. Shared understanding refers to a situation in which the client and therapist are aware of each other's position, and can identify where their positions converge and where they differ. This dimension of therapy is an active process, over the whole course of therapy, rather than as something that occurs only or primarily at the start of therapy. It may even be that the client continues to think about differences between their perspective and that of the therapist long after the end of therapy.

An important facet of the process of arriving at a new or better understanding is the construction of *meaning bridges*. This concept was initially introduced by Honos-Webb and Stiles (1998) to refer to the process, within an individual client, of bringing together ways of making sense of self that had been in conflict. An example of how this can happen in therapy can be found in a study by Brinegar et al. (2006). This intensive case analysis explored the process of therapy in a client who primarily defined herself as someone who took care of others, a position that was in tension with a wish to be taken care of herself. In therapy, this woman was able to identify an episode in her life where her all-consuming caretaker tendency resulted in her pushing away someone who was trying to love and care for her. This moment of insight ('pushing away') allowed her to begin to build a conceptual 'bridge' between two conflicting perspectives on self. This example illustrates how a valuable, and in this instance life-changing understanding can emerge from creating a situation in which the client could make connections between domains of meaning in different areas of their construct system.

In pluralistic therapy, the notion of a 'meaning bridge' is applied to the development of a shared understanding between client and therapist. In practical terms, it is necessary for the therapist and client to arrive at sufficient agreement around the goals, tasks and methods to provide a structure for the work of therapy. It is also necessary that this understanding is grounded in an appreciation and acceptance of the underlying ideas or theories that each of them holds regarding the nature and cause of problems. For example a client may believe that his depression is due to a chemical imbalance in his brain (i.e. a medical model explanation), while his therapist may believe that its main cause is his difficulty in forming close relationships (i.e. a socio-cultural explanation). If it is not addressed, such divergence may cause barriers to working together. However, there are many potential meaning bridges that may be erected, such as the simple idea that one of the consequences of the 'illness' is that it gives the person negative emotions that undermine relationships. Such a bridge offers a way for the therapist and client to find a space in which they can acknowledge the value of taking antidepressants and taking more exercise, while at the same time working on how to develop more satisfying relationships and attending therapy. The robustness of such a bridge might be reinforced by reading Levine (2007), which offers an inclusive, multidimensional understanding of depression.

Becoming more open to the possibility of different ways of thinking may have a therapeutic impact in giving the client a safe experience of dealing with interpersonal difference, and introducing them to perspectives of which they had previously not been aware.

In training and supervision, pluralistic therapists are challenged to remain sensitive to how hard it can be to learn to see issues from a new perspective. Over the course of their careers, therapists tend to devote a great deal of time and personal energy to internalising or 'metabolising' therapy theory to the point that they can appreciate at a deep level how it applies to their life experience (Betan and Binder,

2010). The key learning process here is becoming able to use ideas and theory in ways that make a difference, in a manner that involves much more than merely being cognitively informed about new perspectives. Instead, a lengthy process of personal assimilation needs to take place, in which new ideas connect up with existing constructs. The person needs to be actively engaged in this process, preferably being accompanied by someone else who helps them to see things in a new light by offering personal examples. It is essential for the therapist to be able to reflect on the journey they themselves have followed, to arrive at an understanding of themselves and to allow their clients to have the same type of experience.

# DISTINCTIVE ASPECTS OF THE *PRACTICE* OF PLURALISTIC THERAPY

16

# Beginning

*That was different. I'd been for counselling before, when I was at school. Then, I just met the counsellor and we got started. This time, they sent me a booklet and asked me to answer questions about I want from the counselling, what would be helpful to me, what my strengths are and how many counselling sessions I thought I might need. Certainly made me think. The booklet kept going on about how the counsellor would really want to know about my ideas. And that's what it was like when I met her. She was a nice enough woman. Seemed genuinely interested in what I thought about all that stuff.*

These words are Darren talking to his university tutor, in response to a question about whether he had been to see a counsellor yet. Although Darren was clearly interested in his degree studies, and his assignments had shown a lot of potential, it was clear that he was in trouble – missing classes and labs and visibly shaking with fear if at any stage during a seminar he thought he might be called to speak. The tutor had made a point of talking to Darren after a class, and suggested that he make an appointment at a local community counselling service.

Most therapy is predicated on an assumption that the therapist is highly trained, knowledgeable and skilful in relation to managing the process of therapy, while the client is a person in crisis and in need of assistance who has few, if any, ideas about how to take the therapy process forward. A pluralistic stance invites reconsideration of this core assumption: both client and therapist have important contributions to make. Pluralistic therapy aims to help the client be the best client they can be. This requires consistent attention to engaging the client as an active participant throughout the process of therapy (Bohart and Tallman, 2001; Bohart, 2006).

What happens before the client meets the therapist has an impact on the therapy process, by setting the scene for what might happen in terms of appropriate expectations. On the whole, clients tend to be influenced by cultural images of doctor–patient or teacher–pupil relationships, and do not expect therapy to be a collaborative process that involves their participation in shared decision-making and providing feedback. In addition, at the point of entering therapy, clients may be in a state of personal crisis and emotional exhaustion in which they do not regard themselves as possessing personal strengths and resources. It is therefore valuable to ensure, as far as possible, that the information provided to prospective clients (through websites, leaflets, conversations with receptionists, material in waiting rooms, etc.) conveys the key message that therapy is most likely to be helpful if the client is an active participant. For example, the pre-therapy leaflet provided to Darren at the pluralistically oriented counselling centre he attended included the following statement:

At our service, there are many different ways in which we can help you. We like to think of ourselves as providing you with options, so that you can decide, with our support, the best way to tackle your problem. Some of the issues that clients often choose to focus on are:

- Talking through an issue in order to make sense of what has happened, and to put things in perspective;
- Making sense of a specific problematic event that sticks in your mind;
- Problem-solving, planning and decision-making;
- Changing behaviour patterns that are getting in the way of living the life you want to lead;
- Acquiring new strategies and coping skills;
- Negotiating your way through a life transition or developmental crisis;
- Dealing with difficult feelings and emotions;
- Finding, analysing and acting on information;
- Undoing self-criticism and enhancing self-care; and
- Dealing with difficult or painful relationships.

Other sections of the leaflet invited Darren to think about what he wanted from counselling, and how many sessions he thought he might need. The leaflet included a link to the counselling centre website, which provided brief sections on each of the therapists, and links to further reading on mental health issues and testimonies from previous clients.

The use of language in that leaflet, for example the use of *doing* words, positions the client as active and purposeful, rather than as passive or helpless. This type of constructive positioning also takes place in conversational interaction once therapy is underway. For example, therapeutic metacommunication (discussed in more detail in Chapter 19) is a way of talking in which the therapist comments on what has been said, on what they are thinking about saying or about similar processes occurring in the other person. In effect, this involves standing outside the ongoing flow of conversation, and drawing attention to the intentions that underpin these interactions. Each time this happens, the client receives an implicit message that 'you have something important to offer here.' Although a pluralistic therapist may also straightforwardly tell the client that he or she has something important to offer, the use of metacommunication is a micro-conversational strategy that has a powerful effect through not merely telling, but actively *showing*, this way of relating. Positioning the client as knowledgeable and resourceful is further reinforced during conversations arising from completion of feedback measures (see Chapter 24).

Engaging the client as an active participant requires being responsive to subtle suggestions and initiatives presented by the client. It is unlikely that a client would explicitly say something along the lines of 'I have been thinking about how I deal with my anxiety, and realise that talking to my wife about it seems to be helpful . . . could we explore the implications of this a bit more in our therapy today?' A useful perspective on this process can be found in the innovative moments model developed by Gonçalves, Matos and Santos (2008). Influenced by the narrative therapy tradition, these researchers suggest that much of what clients say in sessions consists of reports on their problems and difficulties. However, it is possible to detect, embedded in the client's talk, moments when the person mentions an exception to their predominantly problem-saturated way of describing their life. These 'innovative moments' can take the form of new actions or behaviours in which the person has resisted their problem, 'protest' against self-defeating behaviour patterns, periods of reflection, reconceptualising their problem and genuinely new personal experiences. This research group has conducted several studies that have demonstrated that therapist responsiveness to innovative moments is associated with positive therapy outcomes (Cardoso et al., 2014; Gonçalves et al., 2016; Matos et al., 2009).

A final approach to supporting client active involvement is through physical props – objects and artefacts that are available to the client. An appropriately written pre-therapy leaflet, or similar information available on a website, is an example of this strategy. Providing clients about information about how to complain, lists of alternative therapy providers and other community resources, and self-help books, articles and websites, represent further ways of reinforcing the idea that the client is making active choices around whether to remain in therapy and how to use it. Such information can be located in a waiting area, on a website or offered to a client at a suitable stage within therapy.

# Therapist style

*As I said before, my name is Sally, and I am one of the counsellors
here. I appreciate how open you have been about how scared you feel
a lot of the time. It was good to hear a bit about the things you have
been able to do to keep that under control. I mentioned earlier that
I would like to say a little bit about myself. If it's OK with you, I'd like
to take a couple of minutes to do that now. For me, as a counsellor,
there are two big things. The first is about being flexible. Different
people find different things helpful. For example, some people who
come to me for counselling want to work out an answer to their
problems, in a logical way. Other people find that it helps to use
counselling to let go of their feelings. The same person might want
one thing at one session, and then a different thing the next week.
Some people just need a couple of meetings to get themselves back
on track. Other people are looking for a counsellor who will support
them over a much longer period, months maybe, to make changes in
their life. I could give other examples. The point is that it's important
to be flexible, and find the right thing for each person. That's why
I am interested in your ideas – you are the only person who can judge
what works for you. Does that make sense? The other big factor is
that you need to feel safe with me. You need to be able to trust me, so
that you can talk about anything at all that is bothering you. Maybe
it will turn out that I am not the right counsellor for you – that even if
I am a great counsellor for other people who see me, there just isn't
a good fit between us, or there is something that gets in the way. For
example, I'm probably old enough to be your mum – maybe that's
a good thing or maybe it's not. If you have any concerns at all that
I'm not the right person, then it's really important to let me know.
I really mean that. Maybe we can find a way to sort it out, or maybe
we decide that it would be best for you to try another counsellor in
the centre. That is a perfectly OK thing to do. Not a problem. I've
gone on for long enough. The last thing is – it's good to ask me any*

*questions that you might have, about who I am, how I see you, or the approach I am taking in our counsellor. Are there any questions at the moment?*

Pluralistic therapists tend to be people who have displayed an enduring lifetime interest around the issue of how to cope with personal problems and challenges and how to grow and develop as a person. This interest may have its origins in a specific personal 'wound', for example a traumatic event in childhood such as abuse or loss. Alternatively, such an interest may arise from a more diffuse range of influences, such as the experience of repeated geographical dislocation or having family members with health or emotional difficulties. Whatever the root cause, the individual becomes someone who experiments with different 'therapies', builds up a first-hand personal knowledge of what they have to offer and is always curious to learn more.

Pluralistic therapists also tend to be people who have had experiences, within their own lives, that have led them to adopt a sceptical, pragmatic and open approach to issues, and willingness to learn about new ideas. For example, they may have grown up in a farming family that was not impressed by fancy theories but only in 'what worked'. Or they may have had a pivotal life experience of training in social work and being exposed to human diversity.

These types of experience connect with current research-based knowledge around the attributes of effective therapists. The 'wounded healer' hypothesis proposes that many therapists are individuals whose early trauma has enabled them to be particularly sensitive to the 'wounds' of others (Zerubavel and Wright, 2012). If such people have been able to resolve their own issues to a sufficient extent, they are able to draw on their personal awareness in helpful ways in their work with clients. On the other hand, if the original trauma has not been resolved, a wounded therapist may be someone who has the potential to harm their clients, by using the client to buttress their own insecurity. The pattern found in many pluralistic therapists can be seen as an extension of the wounded healer model. Pluralistic therapists have not only been able to heal their own wounds (in so far as this is ever possible), but have done so in a manner that has left them with an abiding curiosity around the nature of the change process and how helping interventions work in practice. Life experiences that encourage scepticism and openness to learning also appear to be consistent with studies that have shown that professional self-doubt (Nissen-Lie, Monsen and Ronnestad, 2010) is a key element in therapist effectiveness, and therapist belief that no single theory of therapy offers a sufficient basis for understanding the complexity of human development (Jennings and Skovholt, 1999).

A further aspect of being a pluralistic therapist is learning from the client. If a therapist is committed to working collaboratively with a client, engaging in person-to-person dialogue and being curious about the cultural resources available to the client, then it is inevitable that he or she will learn from the client. Where appropriate, pluralistic therapists may invite their client to teach them about what they know about anxiety, depression or whatever their main problem might be. Pluralistic therapists expect to be surprised by the change process undertaken by clients, and accept that their clients may evaluate therapy in ways that differ from their professional judgement. Pluralistic therapy theory assumes that effective work depends on the ongoing commitment of the therapist to personal learning and development, as outlined in the 'deliberate practice' model (Rousmaniere, 2017). Such commitment gives expression to a positive life attitude that may be of value to the client. It may also contribute to conveying to the client a sense that their therapist is coming to them 'fresh', and regards them as a unique challenge and opportunity. At the same time, commitment to deliberate practice serves to avoid therapist stagnation and burnout.

# 18

# The menu

*You have talked a lot about how you feel safe when you're in your
room, and pretty safe when you're with your mum and dad and
your sister. But meeting with strangers is always hard for you, and
situations where you feel you are being judged, such as a university
seminar, are really, really awful. We have agreed that the first priority
for the counselling is to get to grips with this – in particular to make
it easier to deal with situations at uni so you can finish your degree.
I was wondering if we could talk for a bit now about how you could
deal with these fears – what would make a difference. Do you have
any thoughts, yourself? [No, not really.] All right, if it's OK with you,
I'd like to make some suggestions, based on things that I think might
work. Would that be OK, to do that now? [Yes, definitely.] I'm going
to suggest a few possibilities, and I'd like you to tell me whether any
of them seem like they could be helpful to you. I don't want you to
agree to anything that isn't right for you. If these ideas seem daft,
just tell me, and we'll keep looking. In the end, I'm really sure that
there is something that will work. Also – and I mean this – it could
be that my suggestions trigger your own thoughts about other stuff
that might help. Just chip in if that happens. Right, let's start. I'm
going to begin by talking you through four ways of dealing with fear.
Maybe all of them could help you, or none of them. One thing that
you could do is to learn how to reduce fear when it happens, using
a technique that I could show you, to breathe in a particular way.
That's one possibility, which I think we have touched on already.
A second thing would be that many people have messages in their
head that wind up their fear levels. Like saying to yourself 'I can't
cope', or 'these people are all going to think I'm stupid'. So a second
possibility is to look at what is happening in your head, and learn
new ways of thinking. A third approach is that situations that terrify
you are because something has happened in the past to make you
really sensitive to these scenarios. If that is the case it can be helpful*

*to revisit what happened in the past, so that you can get to a point of accepting that you are a different person now. The final option, for the moment, is to find examples of social situations where you don't feel terrified, that are sort of exceptions to the rule, and to figure out how it is that you are able to cope in these situations and whether these skills can be applied in other situations such as seminar presentations. So, four possibilities to start with. What do you think? Are any of these worth talking about some more? Or even worth trying out?*

To work together in a collaborative manner, then the client needs to know what the therapist has to offer. Here, Sally is initiating a conversation about what she has to offer in relation to Darren's fearfulness in social situations.

In Functional Analytic Psychotherapy (Tsai et al., 2012), the therapist assembles and rehearses a treatment rationale or 'rap' that can be tailored to different clients and situations. Similar strategies exist in narrative therapy (Sween, 1999) and no doubt in other therapy approaches as well. The pluralistic equivalent is conceptualised as a therapist 'menu'. The metaphor of a menu evokes various meanings that can be helpful: the client chooses from the menu; items on the menu can be adapted to meet dietary needs and tastes; tasters and various portion sizes are available; the waiter can explain menu items if the customer is unsure of what they refer to; information can be organised in terms of starters, mains and desserts. As with all aspects of pluralistic therapy, language can be personalised and nuanced. Other possible metaphors include repertoire, palette, toolkit, toy box, playground, skill-set and catalogue. Each of these terms highlights some aspects of the process and downplays other aspects. What is important is to ground what is being talked about in a domain of experience that is familiar to the client.

A therapist menu is likely to incorporate the following ingredients:

- *Micro-skills or counselling skills*. For example, if an important task for a client is to talk about an issue in order to make sense of something that has happened and find meaning, the therapist can offer a repertoire of micro-skills that might be helpful in facilitating this process:

Usually what I do is listen, maybe occasionally ask questions to clarify details and then try to sum up what you have been talking about . . . maybe also reflect back my own feelings that are triggered by what you are saying . . . does that seem OK for you? . . . Maybe we can look at this at the end of the session and see whether its working for you, or whether we need to try a different approach.

- *Ideas, explanatory narratives and ways of conceptualising.* A central aspect of pluralistic therapy is to be able to offer the client alternative perspectives on a problem, usually based on ideas from theories of therapy presented in accessible language and tailored to the individual circumstances of the client.
- *Information.* There are many types of information that may be valuable for clients. This can include research evidence around the effectiveness of various interventions, where the client can find other sources of help in the community, and how different diagnostic terms are defined.
- *Methods and interventions.* Each therapist has their own toolkit of change interventions, such as two-chair work, transference interpretation, experiential focusing, mindfulness, challenging irrational beliefs, dream work, social skills role play training, expressive arts techniques and so on.
- *Cultural resources.* Awareness, and perhaps even first-hand knowledge, of extra-therapeutic activities such as exercise, community involvement, art-making, owning a pet and so on.
- *Personal knowledge and experience.* Each therapist is able to access their own unique personal history for examples of life challenges that they have dealt with, which might be valuable as sources of self-disclosure.
- *Stories, metaphors and images.* Many therapists have a stock of therapeutic stories from well-known movies, novels and fairy tales, and therapeutic metaphors (being on a journey, climbing a mountain, building a house, peeling layers off an onion, etc.).

A crucial aspect of a therapist menu is knowing where the gaps are. For example, a therapist may conclude that Eye Movement

Desensitisation and Reprocessing (EMDR), intensive mindfulness training or a 12-step programme may be helpful for a client, but the therapist may be unable to personally offer these interventions. In such a scenario, it is useful to be able to work with the client around how to access such resources.

It is clear that the information in a typical therapist menu is too extensive to be conveyed on a single occasion, such as a pre-treatment information leaflet or website entry, or an opening 'rap' delivered at a first meeting. Instead, these early introductions to the menu need to be followed by encouragement to the client to ask questions, and feeding-in further information at appropriate moments.

In pluralistic therapy, active use of a menu of options has a number of effects. At the level of the therapist, it supports the therapist's sense of competence and resourcefulness. It is consistent with what Ivey, Ivey and Zalaquett (2010) have characterised as an *intentional* approach to therapy – good therapists function in a reflective manner in which they are aware of different possible responses to a client, and where these options might lead, and are able to select the one that is the most appropriate at that moment. Pluralistic therapy extends this principle by including the client in the decision-making process. At the level of the client, he or she appreciates that the therapist is operating in an above-board and straightforward manner – what is on offer is open to negotiation, discussion and explanation. Because the menu includes many items, there is an implied message that it is fine, and indeed to be expected, that some of what is offered by the therapist will be rejected. This can encourage the client to trust their own judgement about what is helpful and what is not. Finally, the menu implies hope. The client is not being offered a situation where there is one change strategy being offered, and if that does not work there are no options, or they are blamed for 'resisting' change.

19

# Metacommunication

*Can we just hit the pause button? I'm aware that we were talking about how that breathing technique was 'sort of' helpful when you tried it out a couple of times last week. But then it seemed to me that you changed the topic, and started to tell me about your holiday plans. I was just wondering what the connection was. Actually, to be honest, I was wondering whether it was hard to talk about the breathing technique. I wondered whether you might be avoiding telling me that you thought that the breathing was a waste of time. Or maybe something happened during the breathing that was not what you expected? I don't know – I just have a sense that there's some missing bit of the story here. It's fine to talk about holiday plans, but we had prioritised the fear question, and I'd just like to check out where we were with that.*

Metacommunication represents a core skill within a pluralistic approach to therapy, as a means of enabling micro-collaboration at a moment-by-moment level. Metacommunication refers to the act of standing back from the ongoing flow of conversation, and reflecting on (or inviting reflection on) the intentions and/or reactions of the speaker and/or listener. The process of engaging in therapeutic metacommunication is similar to therapist immediacy (Hill et al., 2014), impact disclosure (Kivlighan, 2014), commenting on process (McGrath and Donovan, 2013) and transference interpretation (Ulberg et al., 2014). However, within pluralistic therapy, metacommunication is used more widely, as a general strategy that supports collaboration and shared decision-making. It can also have the function of positioning the client as someone who has valuable information and insights to be contributed, and the therapist as someone who is open to correction.

Historically, the concept of metacommunication was initially developed in the 1950s by Bateson, Watzlawick and other family systems theorists. It was then applied in the context of interpersonal theory, to refer to the process through which a therapist might draw attention to dysfunctional patterns of relating occurring within the therapy relationship (Kiesler, 1988), and then by Safran, Muran and Eubanks-Carter (2011) in the context of the process of repairing ruptures in the therapeutic alliance. Drawing on these influences, Rennie (1998) identified four main types of metacommunication:

1   The speaker may disclose to the other person the *intention* behind what the speaker has said or is about to say.
2   The speaker may disclose his or her reactions to what the other has said (*impact*).
3   The speaker may invite the other to reveal the *intention* behind what the other has said.
4   The speaker may invite the other to disclose his or her reaction to what the speaker has said (*impact*).

Within this framework, metacommunication can be initiated by the therapist or the client. In pluralistic therapy, the terms 'therapeutic metacommunication' or 'metatherapeutic communication' (Cooper, Dryden, Martin and Papayianni, 2016) are used to refer to the purposeful deployment of this strategy by the therapist.

Analysis of therapy transcripts and recordings suggests that, on the whole, most therapists rarely appear to use therapeutic metacommunication. It is a skill that does not come easy, but represents an interactional conversational strategy that therapists need to learn how to implement.

As a therapeutic process, metacommunication has the effect of conveying a sense of respect for the other, willingness to listen to the other, and willingness to be known (sharing intentions and impacts). Therapeutic metacommunication seeks to position the client as knowledgeable and an active agent, and the therapist as 'not-knowing', humble and transparent. The act of metacommunicating functions as a demonstration or modelling of self-observation (Beitman and Soth, 2006), reflective functioning and metacognitive processing, and invites the interlocutor to engage in a similar process.

A central consideration in the use of therapeutic metacommunication in pluralistic therapy is that it is viewed as a fundamental building block in relation to client–therapist collaboration. Rennie (1990) characterised this aspect of metacommunication in the following terms:

> [Metacommunication] exposes each party's plan and strategies for the therapy and opens up the possibility of negotiated and mutual set of plans and strategies; and it gives the client a heightened sense of equality with the therapist which in turn increases the client's personal sense of power and self-esteem.
>
> (Rennie, 1990, pp. 169–170)

By consistently engaging in metacommunication, the therapist strives to ensure maximum alignment around goals, tasks and methods, and how the issues being explored are conceptualised and understood.

While therapeutic metacommunication has been invoked in other forms of therapy as a means of resolving relationship ruptures or impasses, in pluralistic therapy it is employed more broadly as a means of preventing relationship crises. Although the occurrence and then resolution of an alliance rupture has the potential to promote important learning on the part of the client, there are also many situations in which ruptures can lead to the premature ending of therapy. The underlying causes of ruptures are mainly differences in client and therapist perspectives and/or habitual conflictual patterns through which the client typically interacts with others. In pluralistic therapy, the aim is to create an environment where these processes can be identified and discussed as a matter of routine. In particular, acknowledging client–therapist differences (e.g. in style of interacting, values and beliefs about change) is a necessary element of dialogue (Sundet et al., 2016).

In pluralistic therapy, metacommunication is used right from the start of the first meeting. For instance, a therapist might state:

> I would like to know more about what brings you to counselling, and also what is happening in your life more broadly. I will be asking you some questions about all this . . . if at any point you are wondering why I am asking a particular question, or do not want to answer it, then just let me know . . . is that OK?

As therapy unfolds, therapeutic metacommunication might take place at the start of a session, for example around task selection and agenda setting; at the end of a session (conversations around homework, or reviewing progress); and within a session, as part of the ongoing process. Metacommunication may also occur around specific activities, such as reflecting on data from feedback measures and during a case formulation episode. Moments of metacommunication function to pause or punctuate the ongoing track of the client's talk. Too much of this may lead the client to lose their track. It is important, therefore, to maintain an appropriate balance between just talking and inviting reflection on what is happening. Client and therapist tend to find their own rhythm and point of balance over the course of working together.

20

# The bigger picture

*I am trying to build a picture of your life. The difficulties in being with people, particularly at university, are the main thing, but I think it's helpful to be able to place these problems in context, to be able to see the bigger picture. For example, I want to know more about positive bits of your life, not just things that are hard for you. I was wondering if I could take a few minutes now to ask you some questions, so I can learn more about your life as a whole? And then, at the end of the session, if you could stay over in the waiting area for a few minutes and fill in some questionnaires? I don't want to interrupt anything that you strongly want to talk about right now. But if there isn't anything pressing, it would be good if we could do some more of that picture-building that we started last week.*

Any form of therapy involves some type of assessment: the collection of information that is relevant to the process of deciding what happens next. There are five distinctive aspects of assessment in pluralistic therapy (McLeod and McLeod, 2016). First, the information-gathering process is conducted in such a way as to establish a collaborative way of working, and to enable the client to enhance their self-understanding. This typically involves using terminology that makes sense to the client, such as 'building the bigger picture'. Second, assessment is holistic, touching on a wide range of domains of the client's everyday life, and oriented towards the client's strengths and resources as well as their problems. Third, assessment includes identification of the client's goals for therapy. Fourth, it is assumed that the client is assessing the therapist, and will have questions that they wish to ask. Fifth, assessment provides the client with an introduction to feedback tools that will be used through the course of therapy. Taken together, these elements set a pattern of therapy as a collaborative venture.

At a first meeting with a therapist, a client wants to be helped, for example by gaining a sense of emotional release and being understood, or having an opportunity to reflect on a problem and gain perspective. At the same time, the therapist needs to meet the client and begin to build an understanding of who they are and what their life is like, and may also have to agree to arrangements such as meeting times. A pluralistic therapist explicitly acknowledges these dual aspects of the first meeting, for instance by telling the client that they want to hear what the client has to say but will also be asking some questions, and that if the client is puzzled by the questions or does not want to provide certain information, then it is helpful if they say so. This kind of opening statement positions both participants as sharing control. A pluralistic therapist offers commentaries on their intentions (metacommunication), such as:

> You mentioned that life at home was much less stressful than being at university. I think you used the word 'sanctuary' to describe your family home. . . . It would help me to understand all that a bit better if you could tell me a little more about your living situation, such as who you live with, and who are the main people in your life.

From time to time, the therapist punctuates the conversation with responses that begin the process of engaging with the client's issues. This can involve reflecting or summarising their understanding of the meaning of what the client is talking about, asking the client how they make sense of an issue, or sharing some of their own reactions to something the client has said.

Because they are seeking help, a client will usually talk a lot about their problems and distress, and say little about positive aspects of their life. It is therefore important that the therapist takes the initiative in inviting further exploration of these aspects. For example, a client may talk a lot about problems in her marriage, with occasional references to non-problematic relationships with her children. A picture of the strengths and resources of that client may begin to emerge through expressing curiosity: 'what makes it possible for you to have good relationships with your children?' The client may talk about playfulness with her children, or honesty, or having women friends who offer support.

Assessment involves building an understanding of both the inner and outer worlds of the client. In particular, it is necessary to begin to get a sense of the everyday life of the client, for example in terms of what they do at different times of day, who they do it with, and how satisfying these activities are for them. Apart from simply being able to make sense of what the client is talking about, information about everyday contexts feeds into therapy by making it possible jointly to consider how therapy fits into everyday routines. For example, a client who attends early morning therapy sessions before going to work may be inhibited about getting upset because they need to have their 'game face' up and functioning within half an hour of the end of the session. The emotional depth of sessions may be transformed by rescheduling to evening time slots. An understanding of everyday routines also informs decisions that may be made about therapeutic tasks and change methods. For example, a depressed client who is a university student may have the personal time and space to work through a low mood self-help manual. By contrast, another depressed client who is a full-time carer of a mother with dementia is unlikely to have scope to pursue that particular method, or may need to use therapy to look at how to free up personal time to do so.

The term 'therapeutic assessment' is influenced by the work of Finn and Tonsager (2002) and Fischer (2000), who have shown that the collection of assessment information can be done in such a way that it has a therapeutic impact on the client. Within this approach, the therapist or assessor uses standard instruments or activities, such as self-report questionnaires, projective techniques and intelligence tests, but invites the client to interpret the results, as well as sharing their own interpretation. The benefit of using a standard activity is that the therapist develops a rich appreciation of the range of ways that different individuals respond to the same situation or stimulus. In assessment for pluralistic therapy, the first administration of a feedback measure, such as the Clinical Outcomes

Routine Measurement–Outcome Measure (CORE-OM) question-naire or the Outcome Rating Scale (ORS) can be approached from this perspective.

In pluralistic assessment, the therapist shares their interpretation and understanding of the information that has been collected. This takes place on an ongoing basis, for instance by summarising how the therapist makes sense of specific areas or issues, and checking out whether the client agrees. The therapist also makes it clear that they intend to share their whole understanding, and the resulting ideas they have about how they might work together, at a later stage (collaborative case formulation, discussed in the following chapter).

21

# Collaborative case formulation

*The big turning point in the counselling was when we made that diagram of my life on a big sheet of paper. It all just made sense – how things that had become problems had started off as pretty obvious ways of dealing with stuff that had happened earlier in my life, and then become sort of ingrained, like habits. To be honest, it was the bit of the diagram that was not filled in – the future bit – that really choked me up. I know this sounds corny, but for the first time in my life I realised, I actually* saw, *that I could choose to do something different. That it was up to me. And that I had the capacity to make it happen.*
[Follow-up interview, three months after the end of counselling]

Case formulation and case conceptualisation refer to the process of devising an explanatory model, tailored to each individual client, that accounts for the development and maintenance of their problems, and identifies strategies through which constructive change can occur. Most approaches to therapy have developed slightly different styles of case formulation or case conceptualisation, and there exists an extensive literature on how to conduct a case formulation (Eells, 2007, 2015; Johnstone and Dallos, 2014). Case formulation provides a valuable way to develop a coherent understanding of the client's problems, offer the client a way of making sense of their difficulties and arrive at some kind of action plan that makes best use of the time available for therapy. Even many process-oriented approaches to therapy have found it useful to adapt forms of conceptualisation appropriate to their therapeutic aims (Watson, 2010). Within the counselling and psychotherapy profession as a whole, the case formulation perspective has functioned as a source of opposition to diagnosis-driven models that do not take account of individuality and complexity (Johnstone and Dallos, 2014; Persons, 2012).

Pluralistic case formulation is a strategy that is likely to be relevant for most clients, for the reasons outlined earlier. Therapists operating from a pluralistic perspective are encouraged to draw on the case formulation literature to identify formulation techniques that are appropriate to their own way of doing therapy, the needs and preferences of their clients and the constraints of the therapy setting within which they work. Pluralistic case formulation is distinctive in emphasising client–therapist collaboration around the activity of making sense and planning. It is also distinctive in inviting the client to consider multiple perspectives on their problems.

In most therapy approaches, case formulation is worked out by the therapist, perhaps with some input from colleagues, and then presented to the client. Although almost all writers about case formulation emphasise that this needs to be done in a collaborative manner, what they mean is that what they say to the client needs to be framed in a way makes sense to the client and takes account of the client's definition of the problem. This is necessary because without the client's 'consent' (Persons, 2012), it is unlikely that the plan will ever be implemented. Within pluralistic therapy, the situation is quite different. Both the client and the therapist are viewed as having relevant ideas and insights, and the aim is to find the best possible way of bringing these perspectives together. Typically, the therapist may take the lead in tentatively suggesting some different ways of looking at the client's life. The intention is to use these offerings to trigger further client reflection on the topic. Client *disagreement* with what is offered is normally more informative than client agreement. Some pluralistic therapists have found it can be helpful to use drawings, charts and timeline diagrams to externalise and make a record of the shared understanding that is being co-constructed (McLeod and McLeod, 2016). The physical act of sitting side by side, working together on a case formulation diagram, can strengthen the process of collaboration and also make it easier for the client to disagree with the therapist. The existence of a visual representation of the formulation, for instance on a large piece of paper, makes it possible for the client to return to the task on a future occasion and add further detail; it is a way of keeping the formulation open and under revision.

The other main distinctive feature of collaborative case formulation is the incorporation of multiple theoretical narratives and the identification of multiple tracks or task sequences that may be pursued. Research has shown that effective formulations are built around hypotheses that link observations (e.g. information about the client's life, the characteristics of their problems, their strengths) into plausible causal sequences (Eells and Lombart, 2003; Eells et al., 2005). From a pluralistic stance, theories of therapy represent a rich resource in relation to hypotheses and causal sequences. In the formulation process, therefore, a pluralistic therapist will invite the client to 'see' their life and problems through alternative lenses: psychodynamic, cognitive-behavioural, family systems and so forth. The aim here is to find the storyline, or the woven-together combination of story-lines, that allows the client a way of making sense of their difficulties. To be able to facilitate such a process, a pluralistic therapist needs to have internalised theory to a point of being able to talk about it in down-to-earth, non-technical language.

A parallel aspect of pluralistic case formulation involves identifying multiple therapeutic tasks that might be pursued. Some of these tasks may be implied by theoretical perspectives. For example, an account of depression as a process of being locked into negative thought patterns implies that it might be useful to develop more positive thought patterns. Alternatively, viewing depression as a consequence of early loss might imply that it could be valuable to gain insight into what happened, or to work on ways of expanding one's emotional palette. Generating a range of potential change pathways is important for several reasons. It is hope-inducing ('there is more than one way that we can tackle this problem – we will keep going until we find what works best'). It functions as a buttress against therapeutic impasse – if the client runs into a wall with one therapeutic task, it is possible that they are still making good progress in other domains. Most clients tend to see their problems as complex and multifaceted, so it makes a lot of sense to them to be pursuing multiple tracks. Perhaps most significant of all, any formulation in which more than one task is identified and agreed places the client in a position of someone who makes an active choice on what to focus on in each session, or in different parts of a session.

Pluralistic case formulation supports a collaborative therapeutic relationship by staging a therapeutic event or ritual in which the therapist not only puts their cards on the table, but does so in a way that is demonstrably open to correction and energetically curious about the client's way of seeing things.

22

# Goals

*I've been thinking about that goals form that I fill in every week. That number-one goal – 'being able to cope with how terrified I feel in seminars'. I'd like to change the wording of it a little bit. It's still the same thing, but when I think about it, it's now more like 'being able to do justice to myself in seminars, by letting other people see how much I know'. Does that sound too big-headed? Anyway, that's the way I see it now. And, while we're talking about this, there is a new goal I'd like to tack on at the end: 'deciding what to do with the rest of my life'.*

Pluralistic therapy is anchored in explicit shared agreement around the client's goals. Most pluralistic therapists use some kind of goals form that invites the client to list their goals for therapy and regularly rate the extent to which these goals have been attained. Other pluralistic therapists engage in verbal contracting and review along the same lines. In this respect, pluralistic therapy is similar to many other therapy approaches, and corresponds to routine practice in many counselling and psychotherapy clinics. There are two ways in which a pluralistic perspective on working with the client's goals is distinctive. First, pluralistic therapy involves direct linkage between goal identification and what happens on a moment-by-moment basis in therapy by making use of the concepts of therapeutic tasks and methods. Second, pluralistic therapy draws on a multidimensional understanding of the meaning of goals.

Usually, a therapeutic goal that has been identified by a client at the start of therapy is framed in general terms, such as 'to move on from bereavement and make a new life for myself', or 'to be able to be happy rather than depressed'. It is not possible for therapy directly to address this kind of broad agenda, because there is too much to do, and it is hard to know where to start. Instead, it is necessary to break such a general goal into specific tasks. For example, 'being happy rather than depressed' becomes achievable when it is set out as a set of sub-goals, or tasks, such as 'making sense of what triggers my depression', 'developing strategies for responding differently when depression triggers arise' and 'meeting more people, particularly in situations where I can feel relaxed'. In turn, these therapeutic tasks can be accomplished using different methods. For instance, 'making sense of what triggers my depression' may be achieved by keeping a diary, exploring the issue with a therapist or reading books and articles written by individuals who have overcome their depression. This approach to using goal-task-method linkages to ensure that therapy is informed by the client's goals is described in more detail in Cooper and McLeod (2011) and Hanley, Sefi and Ersahin (2016). A therapeutic task represents something that a client and therapist can agree to work on in sessions or between sessions. It provides a specific focus for goal-directed activity.

A multidimensional understanding of the meaning of goals takes a range of perspectives into consideration. There are important options around the language that is used in therapy to talk about goals. For some clients, the term 'goal' may evoke unhelpful experiences of 'management-speak'. Other ways of talking about goals include the use of metaphors such as therapy as a journey with a destination, or therapy as a process of building something new, repairing/retrieving something that is broken or lost or engaging in a project. It is also possible to talk in very low-key terms, such as 'what do you want to get from this?' Some experienced therapists are intentionally highly tentative in the way they discuss goals with their clients, as a means of allowing the meaning and interlocking nature of different goals to emerge over time (Oddli et al., 2014).

With some clients, goals conversations may lead in the direction of exploration of overarching life goals that stretch beyond the person's goals for therapy (Mackrill, 2010). With others, the invitation to identify goals may heighten their awareness that they suppress their own wants, or have been brought up in an environment in which they are not allowed to have dreams for the future. There may be clients whose lives are characterised by internal polarisation or sub-selves, each of which strives for different things. Goals that are identified may be impossible to achieve, or may clash with other goals (Law and Jacob, 2013). These are just some of the potential implications and multiple aspects of consciously engaging in goal-oriented activity in therapy. Other aspects are discussed in Law and Cooper (2017) and Michalak and Holtforth (2006). In practice, underlying issues associated with personal goals may emerge in therapy in the form of difficulties that a client may have in specifying goals, or in sticking to goals that have been agreed (Law and Jacob, 2013).

From a design perspective (Chapter 8), the process of working with goals in therapy can be viewed as similar to that of responding to a 'design brief'. A client who engages an architect to design a new house will have an initial list of what they want, in terms of numbers of rooms, layout and so on. Typically, the architect will then make some preliminary drawings and plans, illustrating what the house might look like. At that stage, the client realises that there are other features that are important to them – a picture window, a dining area big enough for their whole family to eat at once and so forth. Another plan is made, which in turn stimulates further suggestions from the client. It is not that the client does not know what they want in their new house. Instead, some of these wants or goals are implicit, and only emerge once the project begins to take shape. This is what happens in pluralistic therapy. There is always some kind of goal or intention that brings the person into therapy. However, the process of articulating and exploring that goal (or goals) has the effect of enabling the person to learn important things about who they are and what they can become.

23

# Tasks

*It's exciting that you've come up with this aim of doing justice to yourself in seminars. It's like the things you've been doing to manage the fear have worked pretty well and now it's time to take it further. I was thinking that it might be a good idea just to brainstorm a bit, as we've done before, around breaking that aim down into smaller bits that we could work on a step at a time, and then decide which one to start with.*

When a client arrives for the first time, he or she will have some ideas about what they want to get from therapy. Pluralistic therapists pay considerable attention to identifying the client's goals, understanding what these goals mean to the client, tracking goal attainment over the course of therapy and being on the alert for shifts in the way that the client formulates a goal, or when new goals appear on the scene. All this is considered important because it anchors therapy in a shared purpose, and prevents drift into ways of using scarce therapeutic time that are not aligned to that purpose.

Most therapy goals are described in broad terms, and represent general aspirations: being able to be more confident, deciding whether to leave a marriage, finding a more satisfying job, getting rid of obsessive-compulsive disorder (OCD) symptoms and so on. To make progress in relation to goals, it is necessary to break them down into constituent sub-goals or *tasks*. The concept of task plays a key role in therapy, because it represents a way of joining up goals with the techniques, activities or methods employed by therapist and client in their work within a session. It is also significant in that it is the therapist who formulates possible tasks. It may be helpful, as a way of reinforcing a collaborative way of working, to ask the client if they can see ways of breaking down a goal into sub-goals or tasks.

However, it is unlikely that the client will be able to accomplish this, certainly at the start of therapy. It is up to the therapist to suggest possible tasks, and then check out whether they make sense to the client.

In pluralistic therapy, the concept of task was borrowed from research on task analysis, and subsequent model of therapy, developed by Greenberg, Rice and Elliott (1993). Originally this approach was called process-experiential therapy, and was later renamed Emotion Focused Therapy (EFT; Greenberg and Watson, 2005). In EFT, the therapist gains a general sense of the emotional style of the client, and then specifically tries to identify 'micro-marker' indicators of dysfunctional ways of emotional processing occurring here and now in the session. An EFT therapist then invites the client to engage in a therapeutic task designed to facilitate change, right at the moment when the difficult issue has been activated. For example, while Anne was talking about her relationship with her children, her story was regularly punctuated by exclamations of how stupid or insensitive she had been. Her EFT therapist identified these outbursts as indicative of the therapeutic task of coming to terms with a harsh inner critic, and asked if she would be willing to imagine that voice was on another chair, and allow it to speak directly in a dialogue with her (i.e. suggested a method for working on that task).

For pluralistic therapists, the EFT model of identifying and working on tasks has been highly influential. It powerfully demonstrates how subtle non-verbal information, such as posture and tone of voice, can be used in task identification. It also demonstrates how timing can be important – responding at the moment that a marker is exhibited makes it more likely that the underlying issue is live and meaningful for the client. On the other hand, the EFT model of task analysis is overly restrictive for pluralistic therapists, because it is grounded in a particular set of concepts and methods and does not take account of the many other types of markers and tasks that are potentially relevant to clients.

Pluralistic therapy has evolved a set of task categories that reflect common areas of therapeutic focus (Cooper and McLeod, 2011). These include making sense of a puzzling or problematic reaction to a specific situation, finding meaning in life, making a decision and changing one's behaviour. For example, Darren, the client whose case was introduced in Chapter 16, was a student who identified his main therapy goal as overcoming anxiety and panic attacks in university seminars, which had expanded into general anxiety about going to university at all. Darren's therapist proposed that 'it might be helpful to approach this one step at a time', and then tentatively suggested some possible steps:

- Making sense of what this means for you at this point in your life – why now? what are these feelings telling you?
- Trying out some techniques for avoiding becoming anxious, or stopping anxiety in its tracks if it did arise;
- Developing better relationships with fellow students, so that he might feel more supported; and
- Making changes to his diet and (lapsed) fitness regime so he generally felt better in himself and less 'jittery'.

On the whole, these suggestions made sense to Darren, although he did not seem to be completely convinced that meaning-making (suggestion 1) would be all that useful.

Pluralistic therapists working with particular client groups are able to build differentiated problem- and situation-specific task lists, grounded in what they hear from many clients who report similar issues and goals. These lists sensitise therapists to the kinds of steps that might be helpful for a client, and can be built in to information leaflets and worksheets for clients.

Once a list of tasks or task-map has been agreed upon, it opens up several extremely important types of conversation – which task to pursue first, whether a few key tasks should be pursued in parallel, what is the best method for working on the task and how far have we come in our work on this task. A shared understanding of tasks also makes it possible to negotiate a structure for a therapy session or series of sessions. This can take the form of an opening question such as 'what do you want to work on today?' or refer to a task list that was previously agreed. If something comes up during a session, a pluralistic therapist asks whether the client might prefer to suspend whatever work they have been doing, and shift to this new task that has emerged.

A consistent feature of pluralistic therapy is that clients prefer to work on a cluster of tasks in parallel, with the result that a typical session might be divided into two or three segments where a different task is pursued.

The concept of a therapeutic task draws on ideas about the importance in brief therapy of maintaining an explicit focus that allows client and therapist to be clear about what they are trying to achieve at any given moment in therapy. Unlike therapies that focus on one key issue that is taken to underpin all of the client's difficulties, pluralistic therapy encourages a combination of tasks that refer to core identity issues (e.g. what Darren's anxiety means to him) and more delimited behaviour change projects (taking more exercise). This strategy has the effect of making therapy seem more down-to-earth and manageable, and increases the chance of recording gains, particularly early gains that motivate the client to engage more fully with therapy.

# Feedback

*When I filled-in that questionnaire just now [CORE outcome
measure], what really jumped out at me was question 3. What does
it say? Yes, it says 'I have felt I have someone to turn to for support
when needed.' There are some other questions that sort of get at
the same thing, but that is the one that jumped out. It just hit me.
I'm using you for support. Every week I come here and I can talk
to you about whatever is bothering me. But, at least at university,
there's nobody else. That's not helpful. I can't keep coming to see you
forever. So I need to make a life, where I can answer that question in
a different way.*

In recent years, one of the most significant recent innovations in psychotherapy practice has been the use of brief outcome and process
measures on a weekly basis, to monitor progress in therapy, and provide feedback to both the therapist and client regarding whether the
person seeking help is 'on track' towards a good outcome or 'not
on track'. A pluralistic approach perspective embraces the general
principle that feedback measures can make a positive contribution to
therapy practice. However, pluralistic therapy emphasises the multiple possibilities associated with the use of feedback, and encourages sensitivity to how this activity might be helpful or hindering in
individual cases (Tilden and Wampold, 2017).

Most of the literature on feedback measures refers to the application of standard measures such as the Outcome Questionnaire (OQ),
Outcome/Session Rating Scales (ORS; SRS) and CORE-OM. While
these general symptom measures include items that apply to most clients, a pluralistic perspective also invites consideration of measures
with a specific focus. For example, there are readily available brief
scales that assess social anxiety, marital satisfaction, perfectionism

and many other factors that may provide a closer mapping of the difficulties of clients struggling with these issues. Various types of goal attainment scaling, based in the client's own definition of their problem, can be highly sensitive indicators of change in individual cases. Qualitative and visual techniques may make it possible for clients to convey their feelings about experiences that are multifaceted or hard to put into words (McLeod, 2017). The Cooper-Norcross Inventory of Preferences (CNIP; Cooper and Norcross, 2016) allows clients to communicate their wishes around the behaviour of their therapist, for instance whether they would prefer the therapist to provide more structure in sessions, or otherwise. The key point here is that it is important to collect the right kind of feedback for each client, rather than assuming that one feedback tool will necessarily be sufficient.

In pluralistic therapy, the information available from feedback measures is not used from an expert stance, where the therapist is the one who interprets what the scores or reports mean. Rather, measures are viewed as conversational tools (Sundet, 2009). The client's response to a feedback measure is a means of facilitating conversation, where the therapist expresses curiosity around why the client responded in the way they did, and what their views around the implications of their response for how therapy might be made more helpful for them.

Usually, the act of completing a feedback instrument, typically at the start or end of a session (or both), represents a recurring event or ritual within therapy. The therapeutic effect of such episodes may encompass a diversity of change processes. When the therapist treats the event as an opening for conversation, it may be that the client gains a greater sense of agency and purpose in relation to their process of recovery, through being able to articulate possibilities that up to that point had been unsaid. The act of completing a measure may provide an opportunity for reflection – in order to answer questionnaire items, the client is required to pause, scan their experience and summarise or evaluate the meaning of recent life events. The ritual of asking a client to complete a measure, and then taking the results seriously, conveys respect for the client and a message that their therapist is genuinely interested in their point of view. These are just some of the generally helpful processes that may be facilitated through feedback rituals. Some clients may have more idiosyncratic reactions to the task, such as being reminded of humiliating test-taking experiences at school or in psychiatric care. There are also potentially negative aspects of using feedback tools, such as preventing the client from staying with here-and-now feelings or ideas that it would be useful to talk about before they fade from awareness.

A further pluralistic aspect of using feedback tools is that this is not a neutral activity from the point of view of the therapist. Some therapists resent such intrusions into their regular way of being with clients, or may worry that the client's scores may be used by managers as evidence of lack of clinical effectiveness. In addition, the concept of feedback implies that the recipient (the therapist) may receive information that challenges their existing self-perception. This cuts both ways. Some therapists find it hard to hear positive feedback while others struggle to assimilate negative information. Although at one level, the client is just filling in a form, at another level the process may touch on a more fundamental level of I–thou relating. It can be helpful for therapists to visit such issues in supervision or personal therapy.

As a result of the pluralistic emphasis on paying serious heed to client preferences and resources, the therapist is consistently placed in a position of learning from clients. While this process occurs in many therapies, and thus does not represent a distinctive feature of pluralistic therapy, it is nevertheless a significant dimension of a pluralistic way of working. Pluralistic therapists are therefore encouraged to use supervision and peer consultation to review the implications of client feedback for their personal and professional development and training (Rousmaniere et al., 2017).

25

# Cultural resources

*Yes, I did go the Green Party meeting last week. It was awkward and a bit scary. Same old stuff. But I could see that they were doing their best to make me feel welcome. Some of us had a coffee together later. I didn't say much. They were talking about working up a new website to publicise recycling and sustainability issues in the university and surrounding area. I was able to say that I would help. It's just the sort of thing I am interested in, and I know I have something to offer. Going to a planning group meeting tonight.*

The concept of *cultural resource* is a key aspect of the pluralistic approach. A cultural resource is an activity that exists within the personal social niche of the client, which he or she uses as a source of meaning and support. Typical cultural resources include walking, reading books, attending church, having a job, travel, political involvement, looking after a pet, cooking, volunteering and so forth. Most therapy approaches maintain a primary focus on what happens in the therapy room and in the client's account of problems in their everyday life. The influential Lambert model of factors that contribute to therapy outcomes describes the influence of 'extra-therapeutic factors' as making a substantial contribution to the ultimate effect of therapy with a client. Within pluralistic therapy, the concept of cultural resources represents a way of being more explicit about this dimension of therapy, in order to harness its potential.

In adopting a focus on cultural resources, pluralistic therapy is aligned with a broad emerging tradition in psychotherapy that highlights the importance of client strengths. While it is clear that the personal, inner strengths of a client (such as humour or loyalty) are important, from a pluralistic perspective such constructs do not take sufficient account of the interconnectedness and interdependence between individuals, and the social and cultural context of individual lives. A cultural resource is therefore at the same time both a form of personal strength and resilience, and a source of connection to social networks. Conceptually, the idea of cultural resource is informed by theories of social and cultural capital.

From a different perspective, this area of pluralistic work also draws on a substantial amount of evidence regarding the impact on positive mental health and well-being of such factors as exercise, diet, being outdoors, spiritual practice, art-making, and other activities.

A model of cultural resources has been developed within pluralistic therapy to sensitise therapists to issues that may arise in work with clients around this topic. Cultural resources can have a positive or negative impact on the life of the client. For example, working out in the gym for an hour each day may function as a positive means to maintain a sense of well-being and meet other people. On the other hand, it may function to maintain obsessional behaviour, or as part of a pattern of disordered eating. The concept of resource *conservation* makes it possible to understand the possibility that entry into therapy may have been triggered by resource losses, and that a person with depleted resources may find it hard to take risks around rebuilding their resource bank (Hobfoll, 1989). This phenomenon is consistent with the observation that external suggestions around possible therapeutic activities from friends, family members or a therapist (e.g. 'why don't you join a reading group?') are unlikely to be helpful to a client. Instead, the client will find it easier to engage with resources with which they have some existing familiarity, for example things that they did and enjoyed in their childhood (Marley, 2011).

Pluralistic therapists invite clients to reflect on the possibilities associated with cultural resources that are presently available to them, that they have used in the past but have then neglected or that they have never used but are drawn to and would wish to cultivate. For the client, a cultural resource may contribute to internal personal resilience and strength, as well as representing a means of contact with other people, nature and sources of symbolic renewal.

Part of the process of therapy involves using time in sessions to address barriers to the use of cultural resources, and explore the effective engagement with resources in order to accomplish therapeutic goals.

The case of Darren offers several examples of how a pluralistic therapist might work to activate cultural resources. Darren identified many activities that he could join in with or do more of, in the service of accomplishing therapeutic goals. He used a friend in his seminar group as a source of support that helped him to control his anxiety. He went for a workout in the gym before seminars, as a means of filling his body with endorphins and arriving at a state of satisfied exhaustion – both of which functioned as antidotes to panic. He sought out new experiences, through simple activities such as walking rather than taking the tube, as a way of giving him funny little stories that he could use in social encounters. He used his technical and scientific knowledge to gain status in a Green group that gave him opportunities to build close relationships. These activities, small in themselves, each contributed to a redesign of his everyday life in ways that reduced the proportion of negative events and experiences and increased the proportion of positive ones.

Typically, as in the case of Darren, the client engages with the cultural resource between therapy sessions, and reports back to their therapist. However, it is also possible for the therapist to co-participate in the cultural resource with the client (e.g. holding a session outdoors, or watching a movie together), or to collaborate with another person who is a resource (e.g. a joint meeting with the client's school teacher or carer, or their equine therapy facilitator).

For pluralistic therapists, a capacity to activate client cultural resources requires maintaining a personal interest in this topic. For example, a pluralistic therapist might use personal therapy to review their own engagement in resources that are meaningful to them, or take time to learn more about resources that are mentioned by clients. The social justice dimension of their professional role might be expressed through an interest in cultural resources that exist (or do not exist) in the communities in which they work. For instance, a counsellor in a school might support a school drama club, because it functions as a transformative means of self-expression for young people in the school community. The potential significance of different cultural resources may be signalled by leaflets and posters in a therapy waiting room, or links on a therapy centre website.

# 26

# Space

*I'm sure I said something at the start about how it might be useful to keep in mind that there could be other ways we could meet, other than one hour each week in the office. We decided on a weekly email check-in, as well as the scheduled session on a Tuesday morning, and to keep going up until the summer vacation. I was wondering if this was still working for you, or if it could be useful to look at these arrangements again?*

One of the key characteristics of pluralistic practice is a willingness to question all aspects of what happens in therapy, in terms of what the options are and what the client thinks would be helpful. This spirit of openness extends to decisions around where and when therapy sessions take place. It seems to be taken for granted, in most therapy clinics and practices, that therapy sessions last 50–60 minutes, in an office, once a week on the same day and time. By contrast, pluralistic therapists are willing to talk to their clients about other arrangements. For any particular therapist or therapy service, there are practical limits to the amount of flexibility that can be offered. It is essential to be clear about what these limits are. However, there is usually some capacity to consider different possibilities.

The issue of what is involved in designing the best possible space for an individual client, or a set of clients using a service, is not a topic that has received sustained attention within the counselling and psychotherapy literature. Pluralistic therapists seeking to be flexible around practical arrangements therefore need to be willing to do the best they can with the fragments of evidence and professional knowledge that are available.

Time represents an important dimension of any therapeutic space: how often do meetings take place, and how long do they last? There is a deep understanding within the psychoanalytic tradition of the therapeutic possibilities arising from seeing the client four or five times a week. Some therapists are willing to allow clients to schedule the frequency of sessions. For example, Carey (2016) has analysed the effectiveness of inviting clients to have access to his diary (through a receptionist) and select the next available slot that is suitable for them. In this arrangement, a client might opt to return the next day, or to schedule the next meeting for one month into the future. Cummings (2001) has developed a model of intermittent therapy, in which the client is told that they can stop seeing the therapist at any point but are also welcome to re-enter therapy at any point. Oldfield, Salkovskis and Taylor (2011) have experimented with seeing clients for intensive blocks of time (i.e. several consecutive days) rather than spreading the same number of sessions over several weeks. It is clear that some therapists are willing to have ultra-brief sessions with clients who are fearful of being in a room for an hour, but this practice does not seem to have been documented or researched.

Place represents another key dimension. In recent years, there has been a lot of interest in the value of holding therapy sessions out of doors. This approach can include occasionally walking around a park or along a beach for an hour (walk and talk), as an alternative to office-based appointments (Jordan, 2015; Revell and McLeod, 2016). It may also involve extended periods of time in wilderness settings, or engaging in outdoor activities such as abseiling or camping. Being out of doors may change the state of consciousness of the client, and their relationship with the therapist, in ways that can be either helpful or hindering.

Even when therapy is conducted in an office, the design of that space can have important implications for the process of therapy. Some clients may be very sensitive to issues around privacy and confidentiality, and may feel inhibited or even quit therapy if they believe that anyone else might hear them, or see them arriving or leaving. Furnishings can either enable or close down possibilities. For example, there are a lot of ways in which cushions can be used in a session. There are times when a client may benefit from their therapist sitting next to them, rather than face-to-face. There are times when it can be helpful to have a table to make a drawing on, or look at a diagram together. These are just some of the ways in which interior design can make a difference. There is no evidence that a 'perfect' therapy office design exists. Instead, what seems important is that the space is fit for the purpose, and consistent with the personal values and 'menu' of the therapist. The design of a therapeutic space also includes consideration to any waiting area that is used by clients, in terms of the messages it conveys, how welcoming it is, whether it includes information or artwork that might cue the client into a therapeutic process and so on.

There are decisions and options around not just the physical space of therapy but also its virtual space. Face-to-face meetings can be augmented, or even replaced by email contact, phone calls and messages, reminders, access to online resources, a personal web area for each client and various types of virtual reality simulations and games.

For some groups of clients, informal contact outside of scheduled therapy sessions may be a useful element of a psychotherapeutic service. For example, in the field of university and college counselling, there may be students who need help but are extremely apprehensive about making an appointment with a counsellor. In some institutions, counsellors give talks to groups of students and make themselves available afterwards for informal contact. Sometimes, counsellors will run an informal inquiry desk in a student social area, or run workshops for academic staff to assist them in making effective referrals.

A final aspect of designing the best possible therapeutic space is to be aware of multiple possibilities around responding to the failure of a client to turn up for a session. In many therapy services, client non-attendance quickly triggers a set of procedures that lead to the termination of therapy and filling that client's slot with someone from the waiting list. From the point of view of the client, not turning up can mean quite different things, and exhibiting a willingness, from the start of therapy, to consider different options can help the client to find a way back, or even to contact the therapist to confirm that they do not need to come back.

Pluralistic therapy does not advocate that therapists should commit themselves to potentially exhausting negotiations with clients around all these permutations. What is suggested, instead, is that the therapist should be willing to offer some options. The existence of options can be helpful in several ways. It may be that one of the options is something that really is the key that allows that client to benefit from therapy. Also, being invited to consider options places the client in a position of reflecting on what works for them, and what does not. Shared decision-making around practical arrangements can reinforce client agency. Finally, conversations around aspects of the therapeutic frame or boundary that the therapist is *not* willing to negotiate on have the potential to facilitate powerful learning around relationships.

27

# Trying things out

*That was a bit strange. I must admit that I was sceptical about the idea of writing down my dreams. But you sold it to me. It makes sense that dreams might help to unblock me about what I might do after my degree is finished in the summer. Clearly, just going back home and stacking shelves at Asda isn't much of a life plan. So, here's dream number one, which was from Tuesday night. I'll read it out. 'I'm in a tunnel. It's quite deep. I'm looking for a baby. Not sure why, or whose baby it is. I come across a sheep. Then I realise it's a man wearing a sheep skin that covers his head as well.'*

In the world of design, once the designer or design team has begun to explore the brief, they will begin to create prototype solutions – physically tangible mock-ups that can be tried out by different potential users (Brown, 2009). For example, designers working for supermarket chains might create different types of packaging for a product, and invite focus groups to try them out and give feedback. The idea is not to test out anything that might necessarily resemble the final design, but to collect information about what seems to work and, more crucially, what does not. There then follows an iterative process of adapting the design in the light of feedback, until the best fit is achieved. A crucial aspect of this process is that it involves moving beyond talk and words, and shifts instead into creating a physical, realised version of the object or service. The concrete nature of the prototype makes it easier to model complexity, in the sense of 'seeing' or 'grasping' how different aspects function and interact together. It also allows the prototype to be tested in real-life situations or simulations.

In seeking to design the best combination of ideas and methods for each client, pluralistic therapy is influenced by design theory.

**115**

Activities such as prototyping and trying out represent one example of how a design perspective can be applied in therapy practice.

There are several ways in which the general strategy of trying things out can be integrated into therapy:

## *In-session demonstrations*

It can be helpful for a therapist to describe their own experience of dealing with an issue, briefly enact this in the session and then invite the client to join in. For example, Darren's social anxiety had led him to avoid almost all informal contacts with friends. He described a feeling of 'terror' on arriving at a pub to meet his friends. His therapist, Sally, noticed very early on that Darren appeared physically tense as he was talking about this incident, in a way that limited his breathing. She asked if Darren would be willing to try something. The therapist then talked briefly about how she herself used deep, slow breathing to centre herself at such moments, and demonstrated how she did this. She then asked if Darren might be willing to try this out, right there and then. He agreed. Darren reported that the technique might be worthwhile. Within the therapy literature, this kind of intervention would be defined as a specific type of therapist self-disclosure. From a wider perspective, it could be regarded as an example of prototyping, or of improvisational theatre.

## *Evoking a creative approach to everyday situations*

Typically, people develop emotional and relationship difficulties because they habitually repeat action sequences that may have had positive survival value in the past, but that now lead to unhappy and unwelcome outcomes. In pluralistic therapy, it is possible to share this idea with the client, and invite them to begin to find ways to disrupt their everyday routines, to see what happens. This technique is described in the writings of the philosopher and spiritual teacher George Gurdjieff (1963). Darren was intrigued by this notion when it was explained to him, and started to implement it in small ways, reporting back each week to his therapist. One discovery was that walking slowly home from working in the university library, and looking at what he encountered (rather than taking the underground and rushing back as quickly as possible) not only energised him but also gave him things to talk about with his friends.

## Therapist suggestions

A therapist who operates from a pluralistic perspective will always welcome client suggestions around how to work on a problem, and will relish opportunities to engage in shared decision-making around such topics. There are also some situations in which a client has no ideas, and may even explicitly ask the therapist for guidance. In such scenarios, there is a risk that the therapist may fall into a dominant expert position that forecloses on further active engagement on the part of the client. One way of *both* making a suggestion, *and* retaining a collaborative stance, is to frame the suggestion as 'trying out' a new idea or technique to see whether it might be helpful. When Darren struggled to make sense of what he wanted to do with this life, Sally asked him if he ever paid attention to his dreams. He said that he did not. She then briefly offered a rationale for dream work and what it involved, and asked him if he would be interested in trying it out.

## Structured homework tasks

Within cognitive behavioural therapy (CBT) and other therapy approaches, there are many valuable ideas that essentially consist of using behavioural experiments and homework tasks to follow through on therapeutic goals and action plans that have been agreed during the case formulation phase of therapy. These strategies constitute a well-understood version of 'trying things out' that may be highly valuable for many clients as part of a pluralistic approach.

It is important to recognise that, in employing a strategy of trying things out, 'out' primarily refers to the everyday life of the client. The principles of design thinking make it clear that being able to generate brilliant ideas in the office is never enough. What matters is how they play out in real-life situations. The emphasis, in pluralistic therapy, on understanding and mapping the everyday life of the client (the 'bigger picture'), underscores this insight. Constructing prototypes that can be tried out can be viewed as a strategy for making a two-way interconnection between therapy and everyday life.

28

# Persistence

*Apart from the diagram that we made, the other thing that stands
out for me in the therapy is the way that Sally just would not let go.
We spent weeks at the start, gradually getting to grips with my fear,
actually my terror in university seminars, particularly around these
awful presentations they made us do. She came at it from all angles.
Breathing and relaxation exercises – over and over again. I become
the world expert in being able to stop myself whenever I started to
criticise myself in my head. My dad's voice – never good enough.
That absolutely terrible session where she got me to go through being
humiliated in primary school. Painful memories. And then following
up on my own suggestions – going to the gym for a hard workout
before seminars, and making a point of sitting next to someone
I could make small talk with. She was like a Rottweiler – every little
bit of success had to be chalked up. It's funny to think about it now
that it's dealt with. It took weeks.*

Once a therapeutic task has been agreed upon, it becomes a focal
point for work in therapy. For example, a pluralistic therapist typically initiates a conversation at the start of a session, inviting the
client to decide on the task (or tasks) to be pursued, the client's understanding of the progress they have made so far and their hopes for
what can be achieved in the time available. Work on the task is punctuated by metacommunicative checking-out around the client's views
around whether the work is on track. The therapist queries any topic
shifts that appear to represent a divergence from the task in hand.
One way of making sense of this process is that these aspects of pluralistic practice serve the function of ensuring the client consistently
and *persistently* attends to a specific task over the course of a therapy
session (or, for that segment of the session that client and therapist
have agreed to devote to the task). In addition, the client knows that

he or she will be invited to return to the same task, topic or goal at the following session, and may have committed himself or herself to carry out between-session activities relevant to the task. A good example of the importance of persistence in therapy can be found in the case of Cora, a client who was deeply suicidal at the start of therapy and whose therapy patiently repeated key learning messages to her, about her value as a person and her capacity to form satisfying relationships, over a long period (Halvorsen et al., 2016).

A central aspect of therapeutic persistence has been described by Hanna and Puhakka (1991) as *resolute perception*. These theorists have argued that resolute attention represents a vital common factor in effective therapy:

> *Resolute perception* is defined as the steady and deliberate observation of or attending to something that is intimidating, painful, or stultifying with therapeutic intent. Resolute perception can be directed toward anything, whether in one's inner experience or in the environment, that one would ordinarily avoid, shun, withdraw from, or react to. Implicit in this deliberateness and steadiness is an openness to experience what truly and actually is coupled with a readiness to honestly examine it, evaluate it, and, if need be, to change it with therapeutic intent. By *therapeutic intent* is meant that the resoluteness is toward a promotion of well-being variously described as personal growth, adaptive behavior, authenticity, release of stress or tension, and so on.

> (Hanna and Puhakka, 1991, p. 599)

The key argument here is that a person may have the potential capability to deal with an issue, but unless they resolutely 'stick with it', their capabilities will not be effectively harnessed. An important aspect of the role of the therapist is to encourage and support the client in their resolve to face up to some kind of experience or dilemma that they have been avoiding.

A further perspective on this process can be found in research into unconscious goal-directed thinking, problem-solving and decision-making (Dijksterhuis and Strick, 2016). These studies have established that the most effective mode of problem-solving does not involve continuous conscious attention to the task. Instead, the best solutions are generated through a process where periods of conscious attention are interspersed with unconscious thinking. This process has been shown to be particularly effective when the problem is complex and personally meaningful. While the ideas of Dijksterhuis and his colleagues have so far not been applied to psychotherapy, the results of their laboratory studies would appear to support the way that pluralistic therapy (and other therapies) are structured in the form of interspersed conscious and unconscious problem-solving.

These theoretical and research ideas have important implications for pluralistic therapy practice. The job of the therapist becomes that of harnessing the resolute perception of the client on a specific task. Ideally, that task will become a project that becomes part of the client's life as a whole, drawing on whatever resources are available to them, drawing on unconscious as well as conscious resources. What is distinctive about pluralistic therapy, compared to other therapy approaches, is that a great deal of effort is devoted to ensuring that the client is pursuing those tasks that are maximally meaningful for them at that point, maintaining alignment to the task through feedback and metacommunicative checking-out and being able to know when a task has been accomplished.

Finally, the principle of resolute perception serves as an example of both/and thinking. Pluralistic therapy incorporates a range of procedures (e.g. agreeing goals) that are based in conscious, verbal interaction. However, for it to work, there also needs to be space for things to happen outside of awareness. For some therapists and clients, it may make sense to conceptualise unconscious process in psychoanalytic terms. For others, it may be more fruitful to draw on notions of embodied cognition (Claxton, 2015) or implicit dimensions of experience (Carey, Walther and Russell, 2009).

29

# Supervision

*I'd like to talk about the student I've been working with. Young man, science student, really bright, socially isolated, performance anxiety, panic attacks. You will remember I mentioned him before. We have now had 20 sessions. Made a lot of progress with the anxiety. He's basically now able to function in social situations, and each time that happens he feels more confident. So that's worked out quite well. What I'd like to look at is that, now we've moved on to this other big goal of deciding on his next career move, I've started to be really passive. In that open-ended feedback form last week, he said that he felt that the counselling had got stuck. When we talked about it, he said that I wasn't pushing him as much as I had been earlier in therapy. I think he's right. It's something that has come up before, with other clients. When they are deeply unhappy and suffering, I know how to take care of them and patch them up. But then I just expect them to leave the nest and fly away. There's part of me that sort of loses interest.*

Supervision of pluralistic therapy draws on an already substantial literature around theory and research in clinical supervision (Creaner and Timulak, 2016; Hawkins and Shohet, 2012; Lahad, 2002), much of it informed by an open, integrative perspective and readily applicable to pluralistic practice. Pluralistic supervision is distinctive in two main ways: (1) supervision sessions are structured and facilitated in accordance with pluralistic principles, and (2) the supervisee is encouraged to focus on aspects of pluralistic practice (e.g. goals clarification, collaboration, use of feedback) that might be most relevant to their work with a specific client.

At the start of a supervision relationship, a pluralistic supervisor seeks to build an understanding of the bigger picture of the supervisee's therapeutic stance by collecting information around:

- Their learning style;
- Supervision preference (using the Supervision Personalisation Form; Wallace and Cooper, 2015);
- The theories and methods that they draw on in their work;
- Their current personal and professional development agenda; and
- Their relationship with research.

In turn, the supervisee shares their supervision 'menu' and preferences, and together they build a shared understanding of how they might best align themselves with each other.

While remaining open to any issues that might need to be discussed (e.g. ethical, organisational), the focus in pluralistic supervision is mainly on how the therapist's work in a case is informed by pluralistic concepts. The supervisor will typically ask the supervisee to identify areas that might be fruitful for exploration in relation to their difficulties in a case, such as their engagement with goals, tasks, preferences and shared decision-making, their use of different ways of knowing, use of feedback and the quality of their ethical commitment to the client.

The process of reflecting on work with a client may make use of all or some of a series of review questions adapted from Carroll (2007; Carroll and Gilbert, 2011):

- What did you set out to do?
- What happened?
- What went well?
- What went badly?
- What have you learned?
- What would you do differently?
- What have you learned about yourself from your work with this client?

- What are the implications for your ongoing personal and professional development and training?
- What are the implications for how we work together in supervision?

As with other aspects of pluralistic supervision, the model is shared between supervisor and supervisee, and open to negotiation and change.

Pluralistic supervision is similar to any other type of clinical supervision, in seeking to fulfil many functions in relation to supporting professional work (Hawkins and Shohet, 2012). Particular areas of emphasis, and values, that are characteristic of pluralistic supervision are the intention to enable dialogue in which the ideas and resources of both participants can be shared and allow new knowledge to emerge, and the aim of creating conditions under which the fullest possible levels of personal creativity and resourcefulness can be actualised in the supervisee.

30

# Ending

*That picture, it's a selfie I took at the last session – Sally and me. It was her suggestion. And that little box I'm holding – inside it is a little blue and silver button. From an exercise where we did, where she asked me to choose buttons for everyone in my life and lay them out to show how they all related to each other. That button was 'new Darren'. Means a lot. She gave it to me, to help me remember the therapy. We had agreed to give each other a little gift. What did I give her? That was really hard. You can see, just in the corner of the photo, she is holding a mug, says 'best mum'. It's a joke we had.*

The only things that are certain in life are death, taxes, and that any course of therapy will come to an end. A pluralistic perspective invites consideration of the multiple meanings that ending therapy may hold for different clients, and the ways in which ending can contribute to the accomplishment of client goals. As with any other aspect of pluralistic therapy, the aim is to work collaboratively to design an ending that reflects the needs and preferences of each client.

The collaborative structure of pluralistic therapy, in the form of reflection and discussion around information from feedback measures, collaborative case conceptualisation and micro-moments of reflection facilitated by metacommunication, create opportunities to initiate conversations around ending from the outset of therapy. Other opportunities can arise during the process of therapy, for example reflecting on how the client managed during a break from therapy due to illness or a vacation (Råbu and Haavind, 2012; Råbu, Haavind and Binder, 2013). The end of therapy can mean different things – loss, crisis, transformation (Quintana, 1993). These meanings tend to be bound up with a wish to evaluate whether therapy has been helpful. It is also possible that ending therapy may evoke client memories of previous losses or endings.

In terms of maintaining or even enhancing client well-being beyond the end of therapy, it can be useful to consider various processes through which this can take place. Some clients learn to internalise their therapist, as a source of inner wisdom, motivation, support and comfort (Geller and Farber, 1993). Clients may acquire skills in therapy that they are then able to apply in everyday situations after therapy has finished (Moltu et al., 2017). Clients may develop an understanding of themselves and how they respond to stress, or relationships with other people and organisations, that can be similarly applied in future. Many clients are disappointed with aspects of their therapy. It can be helpful to acknowledge this, and look at the future conditions under which unresolved issues might be addressed more effectively.

All of these factors can feed into the design of the best possible ending for each individual client. It is rarely easy for a client to talk about ending. It can also sometimes be hard for the therapist. This is one reason why it can be effective to build an ending plan over a period of time, rather than leaving it until close to the final session. It can be valuable to make use of methods for accessing hidden or difficult material, for example by employing expressive arts techniques or dream work.

There are many creative options around possible structures of final sessions or series of ending sessions. Most frequently, the client and therapist review the journey they have undertaken. It is also usual to agree on the type of ending – final, open return ('I would be happy to see if you if you ever need to consult me in future'), scheduled return at a specified date, agreed future mode of contact (e.g. email, text message) and so forth. From the point of view of the therapist, it can be useful to check out whether it is acceptable to initiate future contact (for instance, to check the client's future progress, or if the therapist wanted to write about the client), and how this might take place. The therapist may also want to ask for feedback around what they did well, and what the client would have wanted them to do differently.

Beyond these activities, there are also more active or high-impact ending activities. Some therapists write a letter to the client, or invite the client to write a letter to a future self (which the therapist may hold on to, and post back to them at an agreed date). Gifts or object exchanges, or taking a photograph, can be powerful ways of acknowledging the bond and keeping it memorable. Sometimes the therapist and client can devise a closing ceremony or ritual, as in the case of Darren and Sally.

In pluralistic therapy, the task of designing an ending is intended to reinforce the core values that inform the approach as a whole – creativity, connection and becoming better able to make a constructive contribution to society.

# References

Allen, J. G. (2012). Reviving plain old therapy. *Psychiatric News*, 47, 3.

Allen, J. G. (2013). *Restoring mentalizing in attachment relationships: Treating trauma with plain old therapy*. Washington, DC: American Psychiatric Association.

Anderson, H. (1996). Reflection on client-professional collaboration. *Family Systems & Health*, 14, 193–206.

Beitman, B. D. and Soth, A. M. (2006). Activation of self-observation: A core process among the psychotherapies. *Journal of Psychotherapy Integration*, 16, 383–397.

Betan, E. J. and Binder, J. L. (2010). Clinical expertise in psychotherapy: How expert therapists use theory in generating case conceptualizations and interventions. *Journal of Contemporary Psychotherapy*, 40, 141–152.

Bohart, A. C. (2006). The active client model. In J. Norcross, L. Beutler and R. Levant (eds) *Evidence-based practices in mental health: Debate and dialogue on the fundamental questions*. Washington, DC: American Psychological Association.

Bohart, A. C. and Tallman, K. (2001). *How clients make therapy work: The process of active self-healing*. Washington, DC: American Psychological Association.

Brinegar, M. G., Salvi, L. M., Stiles, W. B. and Greenberg, L. S. (2006). Building a meaning bridge: Therapeutic progress from problem formulation to understanding. *Journal of Counseling Psychology*, 53, 165–180.

Brown, T. (2009). *Change by design: How design thinking transforms organizations and inspires innovation*. New York: Harper.

Bruner, J. (1986). *Actual minds, possible worlds*. Cambridge, MA: Harvard University Press.

Bruner, J. (1990). *Acts of meaning*. Cambridge, MA: Harvard University Press.

Cardoso, P., Silva, J.R., Gonçalves, M.M. and Duarte, M.E. (2014). Innovative moments and change in Career Construction Counseling. *Journal of Vocational Behavior*, 84, 11–20.

Carey, M., Walther, S. and Russell, S. (2009). The absent but implicit: A map to support therapeutic enquiry. *Family Process*, 48, 319–331.

Carey, T.A. (2016). Boundaries: A pluralistic perspective and illustrative case study of the patient-led approach to appointment scheduling. In M. Cooper and W. Dryden (eds) *Handbook of pluralistic counselling and psychotherapy*. (pp. 288–299). London: Sage.

Carroll, M. (2007). One more time – What is supervision? *Psychotherapy in Australia*, 12, 34–43.

Carroll, M. and Gilbert, M. (2011). *On being a supervisee: Creating learning partnerships* (2nd edn). London: Vukani.

Cartwright, C., Gibson, K. and Read, J. (2016, in press). Personal agency in women's recovery from depression: The impact of antidepressants and women's personal efforts. *Clinical Psychologist.*

Castonguay, L.G. and Hill, C.E. (eds) (2007). *Insight in psychotherapy*. Washington, DC: American Psychological Association.

Chambers, E., Cook, S., Thake, A., Foster, A., Shaw, S., Hutten, R., Parry, G. and Ricketts, T. (2015). The self-management of longer-term depression: Learning from the patient, a qualitative study. *BMC Psychiatry*, 15, 172.

Claxton, G. (2015). *Intelligence in the flesh: Why your mind needs your body much more than it thinks*. New York: Yale University Press.

Cooper, M. (2016). Core counselling methods for pluralistic practice. In M. Cooper and W. Dryden (eds) *The handbook of pluralistic counselling and psychotherapy.* (pp. 80–92). London: Sage.

Cooper, M. and Dryden, W. (eds) (2016). *The handbook of pluralistic counselling and psychotherapy*. London: Sage.

Cooper, M., Dryden, W., Martin, K. and Papayianni, F. (2015). Metatherapeutic communication and shared decision-making. In M. Cooper and W. Dryden (eds) *The handbook of pluralistic counselling and psychotherapy*. (pp. 42–55). London: Sage.

Cooper, M. and McLeod, J. (2011). *Pluralistic counselling and psychotherapy*. London: Sage.

Cooper, M. and Norcross, J.C. (2016). A brief, multidimensional measure of clients' therapy preferences: The Cooper-Norcross Inventory of Preferences (C-NIP). *International Journal of Clinical and Health Psychology*, 16, 87–98.

Cooper, M., Wild, C., van Rijn, B., Ward, T., McLeod, J., Cassar, S., Antoniou, P., Michael, C., Michalitsi, M. and Sreenath, S. (2015). Pluralistic therapy for depression: Acceptability, outcomes and helpful aspects in a multisite study. *Counselling Psychology Review*, 30, 6–20.

Creaner, M. and Timulak, L. (2016). Supervision in pluralistic counseling and psychotherapy. In M. Cooper and W. Dryden (eds) *Handbook of pluralistic counselling and psychotherapy.* (pp. 314–325). London: Sage.

Cummings, N. A. (2001). Interruption, not termination: The model from focused, intermittent psychotherapy throughout the life cycle. *Journal of Psychotherapy in Independent Practice*, 2, 3–18.

De Botton, A. and Armstrong, J. (2013). *Art as therapy*. London: Phaidon Press.

Dijksterhuis, A. and Strick, M. (2016). A case for thinking without consciousness. *Perspectives on Psychological Science*, 11, 117–132.

Duncan, B.L. (2010). Prologue. Saul Rosenzweig: The founder of common factors. In B.L. Duncan, S.D. Miller, B.E. Wampold and M.A. Hubble (eds) *The heart and soul of change. Delivering what works in therapy* (2nd edn). Washington, DC: American Psychological Association.

Duncan, B.L., Miller, S.D. and Sparks, J.A. (2004). *The heroic client: A revolutionary way to improve effectiveness through client directed, outcome informed therapy* (2nd edn). New York: Wiley.

Dundas, I., Anderssen, N., Wormnes, B. and Hauge, H. (2009). Exploring client contribution in a cognitive intervention for test anxiety. *Counselling and Psychotherapy Research*, 9, 86–92.

Eells, T. (ed) (2007). *Handbook of psychotherapy case formulation* (2nd edn). New York: Guilford Press.

Eells, T. (2015). *Integrative evidence-based case formulation in psychotherapy*. Washington, DC: American Psychological Association.

Eells, T.D. and Lombart, K.G. (2003). Case formulation and treatment concepts among novice, experienced and expert cognitive-behavioural and psychodynamic therapists. *Psychotherapy Research*, 13, 187–204.

Eells, T.D., Lombart, K.G., Kendjelic, E.M., Turner, L.C. and Lucas, C.P. (2005). The quality of psychotherapy case formulations: A comparison of expert, experienced, and novice cognitive-behavioral and psychodynamic therapists. *Journal of Consulting and Clinical Psychology*, 73, 579–589.

Finn, S. E. and Tonsager, M. E. (2002). How therapeutic assessment became humanistic. *Humanistic Psychologist*, 30, 10–22.

Fischer, C. T. (2000). Collaborative, individualized assessment. *Journal of Personality Assessment*, 74, 2–14.

Gabriel, L. and Casemore, R. (eds) (2009). *Relational ethics in practice: Narratives from counselling and psychotherapy*. London: Routledge.

Gauntlett, D. (2011). *Making is connecting: The social meaning of creativity*. London: Polity Press.

Geller, J. and Farber, B. (1993). Factors influencing the process of internalization in psychotherapy. *Psychotherapy Research*, 3, 166–180.

Gibson, K. and Cartwright, C. (2013). Agency in young clients' narratives of counseling: "It's whatever you want to make of it". *Journal of Counseling Psychology*, 60, 340–352.

Glasman, D., Finlay, W.M.L. and Brock, D. (2004). Becoming a self-therapist: Using cognitive-behavioural therapy for recurrent depression and/or dysthymia after completing therapy. *Psychology and Psychotherapy: Theory, Research and Practice*, 77, 335–351.

Gompertz, W. (2015). *Think like an artist . . . and lead a more creative, productive life*. London: Penguin.

Gonçalves, M. M., Matos, M. and Santos, A. (2008). Narrative therapy and the nature of "innovative moments" in the construction of change. *Journal of Constructivist Psychology*, 22, 1–23.

Gonçalves, M. M., Ribeiro, A. P., Silva, J. R., Mendes, I. and Sousa, I. (2016). Narrative innovations predict symptom improvement: Studying innovative moments in narrative therapy of depression. *Psychotherapy Research*, 26, 425–435.

Goodman, L. A., Helms, J. E., Latta, R. E., Sparks, E. and Weintraub, S. R. (2004). Training counseling psychologists as social justice agents: Feminist and multicultural principles in action. *Counseling Psychologist*, 32, 793–837.

Greenberg, L. S., Rice, L. N. and Elliott, R. (1993). *Facilitating emotional change: The moment-by-moment process*. New York: Guilford Press.

Greenberg, L. S. and Watson, J. C. (2005). *Emotion focused therapy for depression*. Washington, DC: APA Books.

Gurdjieff, G. I. (1963). *Meetings with remarkable men*. New York: E. P. Dutton.

Halling, S., Kunz, G. and Rowe, J. O. (1994). The contributions of dialogal psychology to phenomenological research. *Journal of Humanistic Psychology*, 34, 109–131.

Halling, S., Leifer, M. and Rowe, J. O. (2006). Emergence of the dialogal approach: Forgiving another. In C. T. Fischer (ed) *Qualitative research methods for psychologists: Introduction through empirical examples.* (pp. 247–276). New York: Academic Press.

Halvorsen, M. S., Benum, K., Haavind, H. and McLeod, J. (2016). A life-saving therapy: The theory-building case of "Cora". *Pragmatic Case Studies in Psychotherapy*, 12(3), 158–193.

Hanley, T., Sefi, A. and Ersahin, Z. (2016). Assessment and formulation in pluralistic counselling and psychotherapy. In M. Cooper and W. Dryden (eds) *Handbook of pluralistic counselling and psychotherapy.* (pp. 28–41). London: Sage.

Hanna, F. J. and Puhakka, K. (1991). When psychotherapy works: Pinpointing an element of change. *Psychotherapy*, 28, 598–607.

Hansen, J. T. (2006). Counseling theories within a postmodernist epistemology: New roles for theories in counseling practice. *Journal of Counseling and Development*, 84, 291–297.

Hawkins, P. and Shohet, R. (2012). *Supervision in the helping professions* (4th edn). Maidenhead: Open University Press.

Hill, C. E., Gelso, C. J., Chui, H., Spangler, P. T., Hummel, A., Huang, T. and Gupta, S. (2014). To be or not to be immediate with clients: The use and perceived effects of immediacy in psychodynamic/interpersonal psychotherapy. *Psychotherapy Research*, 24, 299–315.

Hobfoll, S.E. (1989). Conservation of resources: A new attempt at conceptualizing stress. *American Psychologist*, 44, 513–524.

Hoener, C., Stiles, W. B., Luka, B. J. and Gordon, R. A. (2012). Client experiences of agency in therapy. *Person-Centered & Experiential Psychotherapies*, 11, 64–82.

Honos-Webb, L. and Stiles, W.B. (1998). Reformulation of assimilation analysis in terms of voices. *Psychotherapy*, 35, 23–33.

Ivey, A. E., Ivey, M. B. and Zalaquett, C. (2010). *Intentional interviewing and counseling: Facilitating client development in a multicultural society* (7th edn). Pacific Grove, CA: Brooks/Cole.

Jennings, L. and Skovholt, T. (1999). The cognitive, emotional, and relational characteristics of master therapists. *Journal of Counseling Psychology*, 46, 3–11.

Jennings, L., Sovereign, A., Bottorff, N., Mussell, M. P. and Vye, C. (2005). Nine ethical values of master therapists. *Journal of Mental Health Counseling*, 27, 32–47.

Johnstone, L. and Dallos, R. (eds) (2014). *Formulation in psychology and psychotherapy: Making sense of people's problems* (2nd edn). London: Routledge.

Jordan, M. (2015). *Nature and therapy: Understanding counselling and psychotherapy in outdoor spaces.* London: Routledge.

Kiesler, D. J. (1988). *Therapeutic metacommunication: Therapist impact disclosure as feedback in psychotherapy*. Palo Alto, CA: Consulting Psychologists Press.

Kivlighan, D. M., Jr. (2014). Three important clinical processes in individual and group interpersonal psychotherapy sessions. *Psychotherapy*, 51, 20–24.

Kramer, U. and Stiles, W. B. (2015). The responsiveness problem in psychotherapy: A review of proposed solutions. *Clinical Psychology, Science and Practice*, 22, 277–295.

Lahad, M. (2002). *Creative supervision*. London: Jessica Kingsley.

Lahav, R. (1995). A conceptual framework for philosophical counseling: Worldview interpretation. In R. Lahav and M. da Venza Tillmanns (eds) *Essays on philosophical counselling*. Lanham, MD: University Press of America.

Lambert, M. J. and Cattani, K. (2012). Practice-friendly research review: Collaboration in routine care. *Journal of Clinical Psychology*, 68, 209–220.

Law, D. and Cooper, M. (eds) (2017). *Working with goals in psychotherapy and counselling*. New York: Oxford University Press.

Law, D. and Jacob, J. (2013). *Goals and goal-based outcomes (GBOs): Some useful information* (3rd edn). London: CAMHS Press.

Legare, F. and Thompson-Leduc, P. (2014). Twelve myths about shared decision making. *Patient Education and Counseling*, 96, 281–286.

Levine, B. E. (2007). *Surviving America's depression epidemic: How to find morale, energy, and community in a world gone crazy*. White River Junction, VT: Chelsea Green.

Lowe, C. and Murray, C. (2014). Adult service-users' experiences of trauma-focused cognitive behavioural therapy. *Journal of Contemporary Psychotherapy*, 44, 223–231.

Lyddon, W. J. (1989). Personal epistemology and preference for counseling. *Journal of Counseling Psychology*, 36, 423–429.

Lynch, K. (2007). Love labour as a distinct and non-commodifiable form of care labour. *Sociological Review*, 55, 551–570.

Mackrill, T. (2010). Goal consensus and collaboration in psychotherapy: An existential rationale. *Journal of Humanistic Psychology*, 50, 96–107.

Mahrer, A. R. (2007). If practitioners want new and better methods, shop in the public marketplace. *Journal of Psychotherapy Integration*, 17, 10–32.

Malloch, S. and Trevarthen, C. (eds) (2010). *Communicative musicality: Exploring the basis of human companionship*. New York: Oxford University Press.

Marley, E. (2011). Self-help strategies to reduce emotional distress: What do people do and why? A qualitative study. *Counselling and Psychotherapy Research*, 11, 317–324.

Matos, M., Santos, A., Gonçalves, M. and Martins, C. (2009). Innovative moments and change in narrative therapy. *Psychotherapy Research*, 19, 68–80.

McAdams, D. P. (2013). The psychological self as actor, agent, and author. *Perspectives on Psychological Science*, 8, 272–295.

McGrath, R. E. and Donovan, G. J. (2013). Commenting on process: Highlighting a basic psychotherapeutic technique. *Journal of Psychotherapy Integration*, 23, 193–203.

McLeod, J. (2011). *Qualitative research in counselling and psychotherapy* (2nd edn). London: Sage.

McLeod, J. (2012). What do clients want from therapy? A practice-friendly review of research into client preferences. *European Journal of Psychotherapy and Counselling*, 14, 19–32.

McLeod, J. (2013). *An introduction to counselling* (5th edn). Maidenhead: Open University Press.

McLeod, J. (2016). *Using research in counselling and psychotherapy*. London: Sage.

McLeod, J. (2017). Qualitative methods for routine outcome measurement. In T. Rousmaniere, R. K. Goodyear, S. D. Miller and B. E. Wampold (eds) *The cycle of excellence: Using deliberate practice to improve supervision and training.* (pp. 99–122). New York: Wiley.

McLeod, J. and McLeod, J. (2011). *Counselling skills* (2nd edn). Maidenhead: Open University Press.

McLeod, J. and McLeod, J. (2016). Assessment and formulation in pluralistic counselling and psychotherapy. In M. Cooper and W. Dryden (eds) *The handbook of pluralistic counselling and psychotherapy.* (pp. 15–27). London: Sage.

McLeod, J. and Sundet, R. (2016). Integrative and eclectic approaches and pluralism. In M. Cooper and W. Dryden (eds) *Handbook of pluralistic counselling and psychotherapy.* (pp. 158–170). London: Sage.

Michalak, J. and Holtforth, M. G. (2006). Where do we go from here? The goal perspective in psychotherapy. *Clinical Psychology: Science and Practice*, 13, 346–365.

Moltu, C., Stefansen, J., Nøtnes, J. C., Skjølberg, Å. and Veseth, M. (2017). What are "good outcomes" in public mental health settings? A qualitative exploration of clients' and therapists' experiences. *International Journal of Mental Health Systems*, 11, 12.

Mulley, A., Trimble, C. and Elwyn, G. (2012). *Patients' preferences matter: Stop the silent misdiagnosis.* London: King's Fund.

Neimeyer, G. J., Prichard, S., Lyddon, W. J. and Sherrard, P.A.D. (1993). The role of epistemic style in counseling preference and orientation. *Journal of Counseling and Development,* 71, 5–22.

Nezu, A.M. and Nezu, C.M. (2013). *Problem-solving therapy: A treatment manual.* New York: Springer.

Nissen-Lie, H.A., Monsen, J.T. and Ronnestad, M.H. (2010). Therapist predictors of early patient-rated working alliance: A multilevel approach. *Psychotherapy Research,* 20, 627–646.

Norman, D. (2002). *The design of everyday things.* New York: Basic Books.

Oddli, H.W., McLeod, J., Reichelt, S. and Rønnestad, M.H. (2014). Strategies used by experienced therapists to explore client goals in early sessions of psychotherapy. *European Journal of Psychotherapy & Counselling,* 16, 245–266.

Oddli, H.W. and Rønnestad, M.H. (2012). How experienced therapists introduce the technical aspects in the initial alliance formation: Powerful decision makers supporting clients' agency. *Psychotherapy Research,* 22, 176–193.

Oldfield, V.B., Salkovskis, P.M. and Taylor, T. (2011). Time-intensive cognitive behaviour therapy for obsessive-compulsive disorder: A case series and matched comparison group. *British Journal of Clinical Psychology,* 50, 7–18.

Oliffe, J.L., Ogrodniczuk, J.S., Bottorff, J.L., Johnson, J.L. and Hoyak, K. (2012). "You feel like you can't live anymore": Suicide from the perspectives of Canadian men who experience depression. *Social Science & Medicine,* 74, 506–514.

O'Neill, P. (1998). *Negotiating consent in psychotherapy.* New York: New York University Press.

Paul, G.L. (1967) Strategy of outcome research in psychotherapy. *Journal of Counseling Psychology,* 31, 109–118.

Pearson, M. (2011). Multiple intelligences and the therapeutic alliance: Incorporating multiple intelligence theory and practice into counseling. *European Journal of Psychotherapy and Counselling,* 13, 263–278.

Pearson, M. and O'Brien, P. (2012). Changing views of theory and practice in counselling: Multiple intelligences, eclecticism and the therapeutic alliance. *Psychotherapy and Counselling Journal of Australia,* 1(1). Available online.

Persons, J.B. (2012). *The case formulation approach to cognitive-behavior therapy.* New York: Guilford Press.

Polster, E. (1987). *Every person's life is worth a novel.* New York: Norton.

Quintana, S. M. (1993). Toward an expanded and updated conceptualization of termination: Implications for short-term, individual psychotherapy. *Professional Psychology*, 24, 426–432.

Råbu, M. and Haavind, H. (2012). Coming to an end: A case study of an ambiguous process of ending. *Counselling and Psychotherapy Research*, 12, 109–117.

Råbu, M., Haavind, H. and Binder, P-E. (2013). We have travelled a long distance and sorted out the mess in the drawers: Metaphors for moving toward the end in psychotherapy. *Counselling and Psychotherapy Research*, 13, 71–80.

Rennie, D. L. (1990). Toward a representation of the client's experience of the psychotherapy hour. In G. Lietaer, J. Rombauts and R. Van Balen (eds) *Client-centered and experiential therapy in the nineties.* (pp. 155–172). Leuven: University of Leuven Press.

Rennie, D. L. (1998). *Person-centred counselling: An experiential approach.* London: Sage.

Rescher, N. (1993). *Pluralism: Against the demand for consensus.* Oxford: Oxford University Press.

Revell, S. and McLeod, J. (2016). Experiences of therapists who integrate walk and talk into their professional practice. *Counselling and Psychotherapy Research*, 16, 35–43.

Rhodes, J. and Smith, J. A. (2010). "The top of my head came off": An interpretative phenomenological analysis of the experience of depression. *Counselling Psychology Quarterly*, 23, 399–409.

Ridge, D. and Ziebland, S. (2012). Understanding depression through a "coming out" framework. *Sociology of Health and Illness*, 34, 730–745.

Rousmaniere, T. (2017). *Deliberate practice for psychotherapists. A guide to improving clinical effectiveness.* New York: Routledge.

Rousmaniere, T., Goodyear, R. K., Miller, S. D. and Wampold, B. E. (eds) (2017). *The cycle of excellence: Using deliberate practice to improve supervision and training.* New York: Wiley.

Safran, J. D., Muran, J. and Eubanks-Carter, C. (2011). Repairing alliance ruptures. *Psychotherapy*, 48, 80–87.

Sayre, G. (2005). Toward a therapy for the other. *European Journal of Psychotherapy, Counselling and Health*, 7, 37–47.

Schmid, P. F. (2001). Acknowledgement: the art of responding. Dialogical and ethical perspectives on the challenge of unconditional personal relationships in therapy and beyond. In J. Bozarth and P. Wilkins (eds) *Unconditional positive regard.* (pp. 155–171). Ross-on-Wye: PCCS Books.

Seikkula, J. (2011). Becoming dialogical: Psychotherapy or a way of life? *Australian and New Zealand Journal of Family Therapy*, 32, 179–193.

Sennett, R. (2008). *The craftsman*. London: Allen Lane.

Shay, L.A. and Lafata, J.E. (2015). Where is the evidence? A systematic review of shared decision making and patient outcomes. *Medical Decision Making*, 35, 114–131.

Slife, B.D. and Gantt, E.E. (1999). Methodological pluralism: A framework for psychotherapy research. *Journal of Clinical Psychology*, 55, 1453–1466.

Stiggelbout, A.M., Pieterse, A.H. and De Haes, J.C. (2015). Shared decision making: Concepts, evidence, and practice. *Patient Education and Counseling*, 98, 1172–1179.

Stiles, W.B. (2001). Assimilation of problematic experiences. *Psychotherapy: Theory, Research, Practice and Training*, 38, 462–465.

Stiles, W.B., Honos-Webb, L. and Surko, M. (1998). Responsiveness in psychotherapy. *Clinical Psychology: Science and Practice*, 5, 439–458.

Strong, T. (2000). Six orienting ideas for collaborative counsellors. *European Journal of Psychotherapy, Counselling and Health*, 3, 25–42.

Sundet, R. (2009). Therapeutic collaboration and formalized feedback: Using perspectives from Vygotsky and Bakhtin to shed light on practices in a family therapy unit. *Clinical Child Psychology and Psychiatry*, 15, 81–95.

Sundet, R., Kim, H.S., Ness, O., Borg, M., Karlsson, B. and Biong, S. (2016). Collaboration: Suggested understandings. *Australian and New Zealand Journal of Family Therapy*, 37, 93–104.

Swedberg, R. (2016). Before theory comes theorizing or how to make social science more interesting. *British Journal of Sociology*, 67, 5–32.

Sween, E. (1999). The one-minute question: What is narrative therapy? In D. Denborough and C. White (eds) *Extending narrative therapy: A collection of narrative-based papers.* (pp. 85–97). Adelaide: Dulwich Centre.

Tilden, T. and Wampold, B.E. (eds) (2017). *Routine outcome monitoring in couple and family therapy: The empirically informed therapist*. New York: Springer.

Timulak, L. (2007). Identifying core categories of client-identified impact of helpful events in psychotherapy: A qualitative meta-analysis. *Psychotherapy Research*, 17, 305–314.

Tryon, G.S. (2013). Psychotherapy reflections: What I seek to accomplish in psychotherapy sessions. *Psychotherapy*, 50, 371–375.

Tryon, G.S. and Winograd, G. (2011). Goal consensus and collaboration. *Psychotherapy*, 48, 50–57.

Tsai, M., Kohlenberg, R.J., Kanter, J.W., Holman, G.I. and Loudon, M.P. (2012). *Functional analytic psychotherapy: Distinctive features*. Hove: Routledge.

Ulberg, R., Critchfield, K. L., Amlo, S., Marble, A. and Høglend, P. (2014). Transference interventions and the process between therapist and patient. *Psychotherapy*, 51, 258–269.

Vollmer, B., Grote, J., Lange, R. and Walker, C. (2009). A therapy preferences interview: Empowering clients by offering choices. *Psychotherapy Bulletin*, 44, 33–37.

Wallace, K. and Cooper, M. (2015). Development of supervision personalisation forms: A qualitative study of the dimensions along with supervisors' practice varies. *Counselling and Psychotherapy Research*, 15, 31–40.

Walls, J., McLeod, J. and McLeod, J. (2016). Client preferences in counselling for alcohol problems: A qualitative investigation. *Counselling and Psychotherapy Research*, 16, 109–118.

Watson, J. C. (2010). Case formulation in EFT. *Journal of Psychotherapy Integration*, 20, 89–100.

Whiting, J. B., Nebeker, R. S. and Fife, S. T. (2005). Moral responsiveness and discontinuity in therapy: A qualitative study. *Counseling and Values*, 50, 20–37.

Wilk, K. (2014). Using a pluralistic approach in counselling psychology and psychotherapy practice with diverse clients: Explorations into cultural and religious responsiveness within a Western paradigm. *Counselling Psychology Review*, 29, 16–28.

Willi, J. (1999). *Ecological psychotherapy: Developing by shaping the personal niche*. Seattle: Hogrefe and Huber.

Willi, J., Frei, R. and Gunther, E. (2000). Psychotherapy of panic syndrome: Focusing on ecological aspects of relationships. *American Journal of Psychotherapy*, 54, 226–242.

Wilson, J. and Giddings, L. (2010). Counselling women whose lives have been seriously disrupted by depression: What professional counsellors can learn from New Zealand women's stories of recovery. *New Zealand Journal of Counselling*, 30, 23–39.

Wong, P. T. (ed) (2012). *The human quest for meaning: Theories, research, and applications* (2nd edn). New York: Routledge.

Zerubavel, N. and Wright, M. O. (2012). The dilemma of the wounded healer. *Psychotherapy*, 49, 482–491.

# Index

Milton Keynes UK
Ingram Content Group UK Ltd.
UKHW022030090823
426623UK00007B/20